THE AWAKENING

NOTES

including
- *Life of the Author*
- *List of Characters*
- *Critical Commentaries*
- *Questions for Review*
- *Selected Bibliography*

by
Kay Carey, M.A.
University of Colorado

Cliffs Notes

INCORPORATED

LINCOLN, NEBRASKA 68501

Editor

Gary Carey, M.A.
University of Colorado

Consulting Editor

James L. Roberts, Ph.D.
Department of English
University of Nebraska

ISBN 0-8220-0218-3
© Copyright 1980
by
Cliffs Notes, Inc.
All Rights Reserved
Printed in U.S.A.

1998 Printing

Cliffs Notes, Inc.   Lincoln, Nebraska

CONTENTS

THE AWAKENING
Notes

LIFE OF THE AUTHOR

Kate Chopin was born in 1851 in St. Louis. The city was just beginning to gain a sense of commercial prominence in America, and Chopin's Irish father was ambitious to make a success for himself and his young family in this newly burgeoning American city on the Mississippi River. On Chopin's mother's side, the French influence matched Kate's father's Irish ambition and spirit; in fact, it was the unique combination of these two heritages which molded and fashioned Chopin's unique character.

Chopin's father was killed when she was four, and although his absence was a terrible, empty shock to the family, she was aware that her father had died in an attempt to unite an America that was daily becoming a great nation. His death occurred as the result of an unfortunate accident causing the deaths of several of the city's most influential civic leaders. A key link in the Pacific Railroad was being completed when a catastrophic collapse of a bridge brought the celebration ceremony to a sudden halt.

After her father's death, Chopin was reared by a family of strong women – her mother, her grandmother, and her great-grandmother. They were all iron-willed and capable women, and they all had a strain of the romantic and the raconteur in them; Chopin was often entertained nightly by their many and varied tales of people and adventures.

Chopin met Oscar, her future husband, when she was seventeen. She had just graduated from the St. Louis Academy of the Sacred Heart, and Oscar was eight years older than she; he had left New Orleans to become a clerk in a St. Louis bank. He was immediately fascinated by Chopin's striking beauty and individualism when they met, and the two were soon married.

Not much is known about Oscar, but it is clear that he was not at all Like Léonce Pontellier, the stuffy husband of the heroine of *The Awakening*. Oscar's childhood had not been a happy one (his father was a possessive and jealous man, especially contemptuous of women), and as a result, Chopin was given an immense amount of personal freedom. This was fortunate, for her personality contained a deep desire for liberty that needed fulfillment. She was alive, alert, and excited by the vast opportunities and experiences which life had to offer in her rapidly changing and growing country, and Oscar was always very supportive of his wife's many interests and allowed her even the luxury of solitude – an unheard of luxury in those days, but a necessity to Chopin. Even on her honeymoon, she recorded in her diary the many delights she found in simple walks alone; she enjoyed glimpsing into other people's homes, meeting strangers, and imagining all sorts of histories and intrigues about the people she met. Yet, even with the generous allowance of money and freedom which Oscar gave to her, Chopin constantly rankled at being a woman in what was undeniably a man's world.

The young couple returned from their European honeymoon and lived in New Orleans for their first nine years. Its influence on Chopin's life and her writings is indelible. She absorbed every flavor and every nuance of this exotic American city. And while she was accumulating memories, she was also accumulating a family at the same time. Before Chopin was thirty years old, she was the mother of six children, and she was regarded by all who knew her as a good, thorough, and conscientious mother. Oscar, meanwhile, was having increasing troubles with his job as a cotton commissioner and, in 1880, his business failed so miserably that he was forced to move his wife and family to the small village of Cloutierville in the western, Cajun area of Louisiana. There, he ran a general store and managed a few small plantations, and it was by helping her husband that Chopin grew to love and absorb even more of Louisiana's richly mixed heritage of French, Negro, Spanish, and English ways of living. In this new Cajun country, Chopin adapted rapidly to a society that was strikingly different from the exclusive Creole and aristocratic social worlds of New Orleans. And it was about these people, these Cajuns, or Acadians, that Chopin eventually wrote most of her stories and sketches. It was fertile, untapped literary ore, and Chopin was immediately recognized as a master of interpreting its local color and character. In fact, her early reputation as a "regional writer" is partly responsible for her being ignored as one of America's finest fictional writers. Primarily, however, her lack of lasting, national recognition is due to the reception of her second novel, *The Awakening*, published in 1899. Her earlier novel, *At Fault*, had gotten rather good reviews, though by no means did it receive the acclaim that her short stories had received. But it was *The Awakening* which brought her to the attention of all the major critics and to the general American reading public. Mrs. Kate Chopin had written a scandalous book. Its heroine was a woman who found her husband dull, her married life dreary and confining, and motherhood a bondage she refused to accept. Chopin was blunt about her subject matter, and her critics were equally candid. They were outraged that Chopin had written about a woman who not only had sexual urges and desires, but felt that it was her right to have those drives satisfied. Such novels with similar subjects had been published in Europe, of course, but that was different. A French author could raise literary eyebrows and be tolerated, but because Chopin was American and, moreover, because she was a woman, the critics pounced on both her and her heroine, Edna Pontellier, as being evil and debauched. One critic declared that the novel was "strong drink" and that it should be labeled "poison." Chopin knew that her novel was daring, but she dared to publish it, never dreaming of the extent of furor it would cause. Her friends wrote her many letters of encouragement after its publication, knowing that she would be hurt by the critics' harsh words, but Chopin was more concerned about the book's future than she was about the controversy that it was causing at the moment. When libraries began banning the novel, however, Chopin's spirits sank, and she wrote a note of apology in a local paper. Its tone is courageous and positive and, at the same time, it is wry and satiric. "Having a group of people at my disposal," she wrote, "I thought it might be entertaining (to myself) to throw them together and see what would happen. I never dreamed of Mrs. Pontellier making such a mess of things and working out her own damnation as she did. If I had had the slightest intimation of such a thing I would have excluded her from the company. But when I found out what she was up to, the play was half over and it was then too late." The mocking tone of this overly polite apology is delightful, but it hides Chopin's true disappointment, and when the reviewers continued to attack both her and her novel, she wrote little more;

yet she was never ashamed of the novel or of having written it. She simply felt that she had no further future as a writer. A widow by now, Chopin devoted the rest of her short life to her family.

The Awakening, a first-rate minor masterpiece, has only recently been rediscovered, and it and Chopin's other writings are at last receiving the long-neglected critical acclaim that they deserve. She has been compared to Lawrence, Gide, and Flaubert, yet all her writings and all her characters are distinctively American, remarkably contemporary, and have achieved prominence and recognition far beyond their initial status as romantic, local-color creations.

LIST OF CHARACTERS

Edna Pontellier

A handsome young woman of twenty-eight, she discovers during a summer vacation that she has led a pleasant, pampered married life, but that it has been a rigidly confined existence, and that her husband has always considered her to be his "property." She rebels and tries to find fulfillment for her psychological and social drives, as well as for her sexual drives. She is frustrated because no lifestyle in the 1890s offers her an alternative to the restrictions of motherhood and marriage; as a result, she commits suicide.

Léonce Pontellier

Edna's forty-year-old husband; he has a prosperous brokerage business in New Orleans, adheres strictly to the region's social conventions, and expects his wife to do likewise. All of the Pontelliers' friends consider Léonce to be "a perfect husband."

Robert Lebrun

A charming young man who spends his summers at his mother's resort on Grand Isle making the female guests feel "waited on." He begins an innocent intimacy with Edna Pontellier and flees to Mexico when he discovers that their friendship has turned to love.

Adèle Ratignolle

Edna's confidante at Grand Isle; she is Chopin's example of the perfect Creole "mother-woman." She is a well-organized, busy, home-loving mother of several children, and she thoroughly enjoys her role as a good wife and as a devoted and self-sacrificing mother.

Alcée Arobin

A young New Orleans "man of fashion." He is a good-looking, Casanova-type who is well known for his amorous affairs with vulnerable women. He hopes to make Edna one more of his conquests.

Mademoiselle Reisz

In contrast to Adèle Ratignolle, she offers Edna an alternative to the role of being yet another "mother-woman." The old, unmarried musician has devoted her life to music and is considered to be somewhat eccentric because of her outspoken and candid views. She is genuinely fond of Edna and concerned about her young friend's confused, frustrated dilemma.

Madame Lebrun

After her husband deserts her, she successfully manages to run their summer resort on Grand Isle and support herself and her two sons, Robert and Victor. She is always fresh-looking and pretty, a "bustling" woman – yelling commands to the servants, sewing rapidly at her noisy sewing machine, and clad always in white, her starched skirts crinkling as she comes and goes.

Victor Lebrun

Robert's darkly handsome, spoiled brother; he is also Madame Lebrun's favorite son. At Edna's dinner party, one of her guests garbs Victor in a wreath of roses, and to Edna's wine-heightened senses, he seems to suddenly become the "image of Desire." The vision upsets Edna so greatly that she shatters a wine glass, and her party comes to an early, unexpected conclusion.

Raoul and Etienne Pontellier

Edna and Léonce's children. Edna is criticized unfairly by her husband for neglecting them. Léonce's mother is always anxious for an opportunity to take the children to Iberville so that she can tell them tales of Creole lore and save them from becoming "children of the pavement."

Edna's Father

The old Kentucky colonel did not approve of his daughter's marrying a Catholic and a Creole, and although he and Edna have a good time at the races when he comes to New Orleans for a visit, he is still severely critical of Edna's independence. When he leaves, he instructs Léonce to be more firm with Edna and to treat her with "authority and coercion." His other two daughters, Janet and Margaret, are models of submissive southern womanhood.

Mariequita

A young, pretty Spanish "spitfire" who flirts with both Robert and Victor Lebrun. Robert once gave Victor a sound thrashing for being too familiar with her and for giving the impression that he had "some sort of claim" on her. The young girl usually goes barefoot and is not ashamed of her broad, coarse feet nor the sand between her toes.

Doctor Mandelet

A semi-retired physician in New Orleans whom Léonce consults about his wife's lack of interest in housekeeping and her notions about the "eternal rights of women." Doctor Mandelet, who has a "reputation for wisdom rather than skill," advises Léonce to be patient and not to worry. To him, Edna is going through a "mood" that will soon pass.

Montel

A friend of the Lebrun family and unofficial beau of Madame Lebrun; he hires Robert for a position in his firm in Vera Cruz, Mexico.

Madame Antoine

Robert brings Edna to her house to rest after Edna has to leave Mass because of the oppressive heat and Edna's emotional exhaustion; she lives with her son, Tonie.

Mrs. James Highcamp

A devotee of the races and friend of Alcée Arobin.

CRITICAL COMMENTARIES

CHAPTER 1

The novel opens on a Sunday in summer, in the late nineteenth century. A New Orleans businessman and his wife are vacationing on Grand Isle, a popular Creole resort, fifty miles south of New Orleans. Mr. Léonce Pontellier is irritated by the mid-morning chatter of birds, his landlady's shrill commands to her staff, and a particularly noisy piano duet played by two children; he is anxious to return to his brokerage business in the city. His wife is swimming.

This Sunday tableau is typical of many American and British novels of that era. In such novels, the setting was described, and after the main characters were introduced, the action began. Chopin's structure for *The Awakening* fits this scheme, but she embellishes her narrative skeleton with a multitude of details that her enthusiastic, early critics labeled as "local color." To the critics and readers not familiar with the region, New Orleans and its Creole trappings were mysterious and exotic. Chopin, for example, begins her novel with a stylistic flourish: "A green and yellow parrot, which hung in a cage outside the door, kept repeating over and over: *'Allez vous-en! Allez vous-en! Sapristi!'* " Put in a historical context, this was a rather bold stylistic stroke for a female novelist, especially one who wanted to be taken seriously and whose theme in this novel is the discontent and revolt of a woman who refuses to pay the price that matrimony and motherhood demand.

The caged parrot, however, is not merely "local color," nor is the caged mocking bird on the other side of the doorway mere decoration. Both are symbols of the novel's heroine, Edna Pontellier, who will "awaken" in the novel and discover that she is caged in a marriage that does not allow her to grow or to become a mature, self-critical woman with a mind of her own and a sexual body of her own. Interestingly, Edna Pontellier's husband is only mildly irritated by the noise of the caged parrot; later in the novel, he will be confused and furious when he finds himself threatened by a wife who tells him that she refuses, as it were, to parrot the "right" phrases and refuses to perform what is expected of the wife of a well-to-do businessman. For the present, the caged birds which hang on either side of the resort doorway seem only a part of Chopin's local color, and we should realize now that she will thread them and many other motifs throughout her novel to give it dimension and texture.

The other local color accents in this first chapter – in addition to the French- and Spanish-speaking parrot and the summer resort being south of New Orleans – are the Creole landlady dressed in starched, crinkled white (a contrast to the silent lady dressed in black, walking among the cabins and saying her rosary), the nearby island of Chênière Caminada, where Sunday mass is given, and the Pontellier's quadroon nurse, who follows the Pontelliers' two children around. Similar details frequently appear in Chopin's fiction; critics noted them and praised them. Yet it was not until *The Awakening* was published that they began to seriously consider the inner lives of the characters who lived in the midst of all this local color. Because Chopin was southern, and also a woman, critics read her short stories and pronounced them to be "finished," "charming," "delicious," and one even noted that she had "the dialect 'down fine.' " But *The Awakening* changed all that because the heroine is a woman who painfully comes to realize that many of the satisfactions of life are denied to her – precisely because she is a woman. Edna's awakening to the fact that she has no real identity and her subsequent revolt against this stifling southern status quo alarmed most of the readers and certainly all of the critics. The novel was said to be scandalous, and it was neglected and largely forgotten. Today, however, it has been recognized as a minor masterpiece, one of those small classics that is good literature and a joy to read and reread.

In Chapter 1, Chopin introduces us, first of all, to Edna's husband, and we hear about Edna from him before we see her for ourselves and are able to form our own impression. The man that Edna married is rather slender, has straight brown hair (parted neatly), a precisely trimmed beard, a slight stoop, and is forty years old. He is uncomfortable during this lazy summer weekend and is anxious to return to his business dealings in New Orleans. His first utterance is an "exclamation of disgust."

When we first see Edna through Mr. Pontellier's eyes, she is at a distance, and it is not precisely Edna whom we see. Far down on the beach we see only a white sunshade, or parasol, approaching. Under it are Edna and young Robert Lebrun, the landlady's son, whom Edna finds unusually fascinating. The mood of the lazy Sunday permeates this chapter as Chopin describes Edna's parasol approaching at a snail's pace, the gulf itself "melting hazily" into the horizon, and Edna and Robert seating themselves with "some appearance of fatigue," as they lean against the cottage posts. Mr. Pontellier says that it is "folly" to have gone swimming in such heat. His stuffy reaction reveals his characteristic indignation at his wife's childish and unladylike immaturity. He, of course, took a swim at the "proper" hour, at daybreak, and that is precisely why the morning has seemed long and never-ending to him. He feels out of place in this relaxed and peaceful pattern of his wife's Sunday morning, in the same way that he felt distracted by the early, noisy bustle around the Lebrun cottage.

"You are burnt beyond recognition," Léonce says to Edna. In other words, Edna has broken the social code which measures a woman's respectability by the cut of her dress, the length of her gloves, and in this case, by the color of her complexion. Edna is almost as dark as the racially mixed servants at the Lebruns' summer resort. Chopin then tells us precisely what Mr. Pontellier thinks of his wife: Léonce Pontellier regards Edna as "a valuable piece of personal property that has suffered some damage." Here is the key to Edna's predicament. Later in the novel, she will discover that she cannot be anyone's "personal property"; she cannot be the personal property of her husband or even of her children. She will refuse to be restricted by society, by her husband's code of confinement, or by the demands of her children.

Yet at this moment, when we first view Edna, she does not seem to feel particularly restricted by convention or by her husband's callous remark. She is enjoying the summer heat, the swimming, and she enjoys being the relaxed companion of young Robert Lebrun. When Edna is swimming, she is free of all bonds on her. She even takes off her wedding rings before she goes swimming – and she does this in an age when most married women superstitiously never removed their wedding rings. Here, she blithely takes them off, and she delights like a child when she asks for her rings back, slips them on, and watches them sparkle on her tanned fingers. Note here that when she wishes to have her rings, Edna and her husband do not exchange a word. They have lived together long enough to anticipate one another's requests and to respond to one another's gestures. Mr. Pontellier understands what Edna wants when she raises her hands; later, she understands what he means when he shrugs an answer to one of her questions.

In her husband's opinion, Edna is a good wife, if a bit irresponsible. He is so confident of her faithfulness that he is neither irritated nor jealous at the pleasure she finds in the company of Robert Lebrun. But instead of swimming and joking with the boyish Lebrun, Mr. Pontellier would much prefer to be playing billiards with other men.

The first scene closes with Edna asking her husband if he is coming to dinner. He doesn't give her an answer; he shrugs his shoulders, and Edna accepts his non-verbal communication and "understands." Again, her prescribed role does not seemingly bother her too much. Léonce allows her the freedom to go swimming, provides a nurse to look after their children, and gives her the freedom to enjoy Robert's company. Her husband's indifference doesn't bother her unduly. The prosaic reality of her marriage has become a habit, as has her passive response to it. As we might expect in any well-constructed novel entitled *The Awakening*, the heroine will first be viewed "asleep," as it were, before her "awakening" occurs. This is exactly what Chopin has done in this first chapter. She has shown us Edna Pontellier, and she has richly described Edna's two worlds—her exterior world (as a wife and mother) and her interior world (as a woman asleep—emotionally, intellectually, spiritually, and sexually), and the walls of both these worlds will topple before the novel is finished.

CHAPTERS 2-4

By choosing, first of all, to describe Edna's eyes (the "mirrors of the soul" in nineteenth century literature), Chopin tells us precisely what Edna looks like and *how* she looks: Edna is a handsome woman, rather than a beautiful one. Her eyebrows are thick and horizontal, and the eyes themselves are the same yellow-brown color of her hair; they fasten onto an object and hold it. Edna's gaze is candid and frank, yet contemplative, and Chopin's description here is direct and clearcut, very much like Edna herself.

After Edna's husband leaves for his club, Chopin focuses on Edna and Robert Lebrun, the young man whom Edna finds engaging. From Chopin's details, we realize that although Robert is the landlady's son, he himself isn't particularly well-to-do. He rolls his own cigarettes, for instance, because he can't afford cigars; the cigar which he has in his pocket is a gift from Edna's husband, a treat he has reserved for himself after dinner. Robert's youth is accented by his clean-shaven face, in contrast to Mr. Pontellier's bearded features, which fashionably connote money and status. Robert has a boyish air, and as we learn later, he is not terribly ambitious. We also learn later that Robert has a modest job in New Orleans as a clerk; there, his fluency in English, French, and Spanish is highly valued. Robert seems to drift through life; he is drifting this summer, as he has done for many summers, hoping something will happen to make this summer interesting, and Edna's presence, it would seem, has just accomplished that.

Robert's most prominent feature is his facial *expression*: his is one of open contentment, where "there rested no shadow of care." Edna's eyes contemplate, Chopin tells us, "lost in an inward gaze"; Robert's eyes reflect "the light and languor of the summer day." Chopin inserts an abundance of description here in order to slowly create a mood. Earlier, her tempo was busily paced to catch our initial interest. We looked at, listened to, and noted Mr. Pontellier's impatience and his disgust at the noisy birds, the soprano cawings of his landlady, and the piano duet by the Farival twins. Now Chopin shifts this scene to an andante mood as she leisurely delineates two central charac- ters—two people who value leisure, as they share the summer warmth of the Gulf and one another's presence. Edna plays with a palm-leaf fan, and she and Robert talk lightly about inconsequential things— the breeze, the pleasure they had while swimming, and the Pontellier children—all of the things that disgruntled Mr. Pontellier. The scene Chopin describes is a scene designed for lovers—which Edna and Robert are not, yet.

Throughout this novel, Chopin is never far from her narrative, and the early critics who charged her with "letting her stories tell them- selves" or, on the other hand, of writing "analytical studies" failed to discern her particular style. One of the delights of reading Chopin's fiction is being suddenly aware, now and then, that we are hearing Chopin herself as she presents her characters and their problems. As an example, listen to her as she tells us about Robert: Robert "talked a good deal about himself. He was very young, and did not know any better. Mrs. Pontellier talked a little about herself for the same reason." The effect is dazzling. Chopin is being humorously intimate with us, while employing economy, conciseness, and a certain wise, wry humor. We have the feeling that she has a good understanding of her characters and knows and cares about the minor foibles of these young people. The effect is similar to Henry James' portraits, especially as she continues her description and tells us that Robert spoke of his intention of "going to Mexico in the summer, where fortune awaited him." Then Chopin offers us this neatly packed perception: Robert "was always intending to go to Mexico, but some way never got there." Succinct statements like this are electric with importance; we can predictably expect Robert either to continue his long-delayed daydream of seeking his fortune in Mexico, or else he may dramatically decide to stop his drifting and actually leave for Mexico. Already she has created suspense for us.

Edna and Robert's parting near dinnertime is casual; Chopin sustains the languid mood of the afternoon as Edna rises and goes to her room, and Robert joins Edna's children for a few last moments of play. There is a peaceful naivete in the simple pleasure that Robert and Edna find in one another. Neither of them, of course, is aware that they have begun an innocent intimacy.

The charm of Chopin's introduction to the Lebruns' summer resort on Grand Isle and to the typical upper-middle-class Pontelliers abruptly ends when Léonce Pontellier returns late from his club and loudly reproaches his wife for her "habitual neglect of the children." His loud anger is unjustified; his railing at Edna is not motivated by his concern for the boys or by young Raoul's questionable fever. In this scene, Léonce acts "like a child," a patronizing accusation which he frequently levels at Edna. He arrives home late, in high spirits, and expects Edna, "the sole object of his existence," as he likes to brag about her, to be awake and to adoringly listen to every word of his brusque joking about what happened at the club. He is angry that Edna is asleep, and he chooses to punish her with unwarranted charges that she is an irresponsible and negligent mother.

It is a temptation to make an easy villain of Léonce Pontellier. But he is no villain; in today's jargon, he is merely another example of a male chauvinist, a role not at all uncommon in his era. Léonce dramatically leaves the room of his allegedly sick child and orders his wife to tend to the child; meanwhile, he puffs on a cigar. His noisy concern for the child is enough responsibility for him in his role as a father and a husband. His responsibilities are practical; his duties include the brokerage business and making a living for the family. He has no time to either worry about his children's health or tend to their illnesses. Léonce believes both duties to be "a mother's place."

In this scene, it is significant that Chopin does not insert an editorial voice into the narrative. She presents the conflict between the Pontelliers quickly and cleanly. Instead of didactically denouncing Léonce's unjust actions, Chopin focuses more on Edna; she explores Edna's feelings after Léonce has finished his cigar and has fallen asleep. Edna is bewildered – and not merely about her husband's unjust outburst. She does not understand why she is suddenly crying; the fact that she is crying disturbs her more than her husband's angry insults. She feels lost but she is not absolutely lost; in particular, she is aware that she is allowing herself to succumb to a strange, deep mood. This is the first time that such heavy emotion has overwhelmed her and that she has let herself be *aware* that she is dissatisfied with her marriage and with Léonce. Her confusion dissolves her. She is slowly awakening in this sense. Until now, Léonce's upbraidings have never mattered particularly; Léonce has always been abundantly kind and devoted, as a generous recompense for her service to him as a wife and as a mother to his children. But tonight something new and different has suddenly happened, and Edna cannot fathom her strange sense of oppression nor does she even try to. It comes from "some unfamiliar part of her consciousness"; its anguish is vague, "strange and unfamiliar," and it consumes her. Of central importance is the fact that she *allows* herself to be engulfed in emotion.

Next morning, Mr. Pontellier leaves punctually in his carriage to catch the steamer to New Orleans; he will not return to Grand Isle until the following Saturday. Chopin, therefore, neatly concludes this chapter with a tableau of his leaving. Léonce's excitement builds as he anticipates a lively business week ahead of him, and he gives Edna half of his night's winnings as he leaves.

The effect of Léonce's leaving is liberating to Edna. Yet this feeling vanishes in a few days; Edna receives a box of candies from him, and the values of her mother and her grandmother and long generations of women before her cause her to graciously acknowledge that Léonce *is* a good man. Léonce gives Edna things; he is overly generous with presents to her. Edna is envied; people say that Mr. Pontellier is the best husband in the world. Not surprisingly, Edna decides that perhaps, after all, Léonce is a fine husband. Chopin's final comment here is that Edna "was forced to admit that she knew of none better"—that is, Edna knew of no better husband than Léonce. Perhaps this is true; perhaps Edna does not know of a better husband, but earlier in this scene we witnessed Edna beginning to feel the possibility that there *might* be something more to marriage than what she and Léonce share, something deeper in the relationship between a man and a woman than that which exists between her and Léonce. A sense of dissatisfaction, undefined and indistinct as of yet, has taken root unconsciously within her.

Perhaps some of this has to do with the setting. Compared to the rest of the women on Grand Isle, Edna is different. On the surface, Edna is a "good" mother and a "good" wife, but not in the way that Léonce, for example, is a "perfect" husband. Edna is not what Léonce expects her to be—that is, she is not like the "mother-women" here at Grand Isle. This term that Chopin uses to describe the Creole women is superlative, and its concept is central to the novel's theme. In the following chapters, we see Edna mingling with the other women and, as she does so, we measure her against them. Grand Isle, it is clear, is a summer nesting place for mother-women while their husbands are working in New Orleans. One can see them fluttering about the resort, their protective wings protecting their brood of children. But not Edna. Her boys fight their own battles, overseen by their quadroon nurse who, when need be, buttons trousers for the boys and makes sure that their hair is parted on the proper side—all the little things that the mother-women do for their children.

As a perfect example of this mother-woman, there is none better than Edna's good friend, Adèle Ratignolle. Whereas Edna is handsome, Adèle is strikingly beautiful. Edna's yellow-brown hair contrasts with Adèle's spun-gold hair that neither "comb nor confining pin" can restrain. Mothering, like her golden good looks, comes as easily and as regularly to Adèle as her continual birthing of babies. Nor does mothering seem to drain her energy. Adèle radiates gifted capability, whether she is tending her children or mending one of their bibs. Chopin captures the essence of Adèle as the mother-woman marvels over a pattern for a baby's winter drawers. Edna, in contrast, could not be less interested. She has never felt an impromptu, bubbling joy over the intricacies of a baby's winter drawers. She is capable of joy, but not about next season's baby clothes, and it bothers her that she feels that she should at least feign an interest in such things simply because she is a mother.

Although Edna has never taken the time to analyze her thoughts, she is aware that it is impolite to act uninterested in a friend's enthusiasms. But Adèle's passion for motherhood is only one of many things which Edna cannot explain or feel comfortable with. Equally puzzling is the Creole temperament. Edna Pontellier is the only non-Creole at Grand Isle, and she is not used to the community bond that exists among them—in particular, their "entire absence of prudery" and their "freedom of expression." These people have grand emotions—real and feigned—and share their feelings with the community; Edna does not. Her joys and her disappointments in life have been brief and certainly never tumultuous; usually she is evenly felicitious and somewhat guarded. Adèle can talk easily about a woman's "condition"; Edna is not even at ease when using this euphemism to describe a woman's pregnancy. Edna is bored with Adèle's patterns and she is shy about sexual matters. In contrast to the mother-women, Edna is a lady-child. But this summer, Edna is changing—a bit. She is astonished at the Creoles' frankness and their freedom of expression; the risque books and stories which make the rounds of the guests amaze her sense of privacy. But she slowly begins to realize that their world is not a threat to her own and that their world is made up of wonders "which never cease." To a certain degree, all of this fascinates her.

But what Edna does not realize—yet—is that these women, while being free to discuss sexual matters, have given up their own unique identities. Their freedom to talk about sexual matters is natural to them because of its being relevant to marriage and children. They seem free, yet all of them have willingly conformed to the prescribed role pattern for the Creole wife and mother. Their frankness is not unusual to them; it is something they grew up with. And this frankness is not synonymous with freedom. Their frankness about sex and sexuality is merely a part of their evolving into mother-women; moreover, they have all conformed willingly. Edna feels alien because she could never conform so willingly to their role. She has conformed, certainly, for she has a prudish side; she was reared to be a "lady." But Edna is also somewhat of an innocent, childlike rebel. She is most unladylike, at times, because she swims at whatever hour of the day she wants to, doesn't worry about how brown her skin becomes, and she is more than willing to let a quadroon nurse look after her children. In fact, it is her very individuality which is most striking about her, compared with the other women of Grand Isle.

CHAPTERS 5-6

Because Edna is not one of the Creoles, she often watches them with a sense of fascinated detachment; for example, she thoroughly enjoys young Robert Lebrun's company, but her friendship with Robert is not as open nor as close as is Adèle's friendship with him. Adèle and Robert share a playful, spirited camaraderie. They joke, in Edna's presence, about Robert's "role" at Grand Isle; for the last two summers, Robert was Mademoiselle Duvigne's "knight" of sorts – that is, he pretended to be ready to serve her every whim, and he pretended to be inconsolable if her temper darkened. After Mademoiselle Duvigne died, Robert posed as the very figure of despair at the feet of Adèle, grateful for any crumbs of sympathy she might toss to him in his depression. It was a game of fantasy and romance for Robert and Adèle, fraught with gestures of grand emotions and grand passions – sensations which are alien to Edna. She sits on the edge of their mirth as they delight in teasing one another about broken hearts and tragic sufferings.

This scene helps us to better understand the "exotic" Creoles. Chopin wanted to show us the light and easy familiarity that existed between married Creole women and single men. The mere idea of jealousy makes Adèle and Robert laugh; the community shares its joys and its sorrows with all its members. And sexual jealousy for the Creoles, Chopin tells us, is virtually unknown. Jealousy, she says, is that "gangrene passion . . . which has become dwarfed by disuse." Chopin's comment here reminds us of Léonce Pontellier's attitude toward Robert; he feels absolutely no jealousy toward the young man. Likewise, Adèle's husband is not jealous of Robert and, therefore, this particular scene between Adèle and Robert should be compared to the scenes between Robert and Edna. The relationship between the young Creole man and Edna, the outsider, is "different." Robert does not feel free to exaggerate and boldly joke with her about "passions" which burn within him until "the very sea sizzled when he took his daily plunge." Throughout this novel, we must be continually aware that Edna is not a Creole; she has never experienced passion – real or imagined – nor has she ever discussed it nor joked lightheartedly with anyone about it, especially the "hopeless passion" which Robert describes himself as being a tragic victim of.

This light bantering about "hopeless passion" is important to note here, for it is not wholly comic nor merely a part of Chopin's "local color"; it is an element which will play a pivotal role later in the novel when Edna becomes a victim of a passion that is, as it turns out, hopeless. Yet, at this moment, passion is a subject of romantic comedy, and while Adèle can laugh gaily at Robert's rich inventiveness, Edna cannot; she has never tossed through sleepless nights because of "consuming flames." She soon will, however, and thus, Chopin is preparing us for the change that is about to occur within Edna by showing us how foreign these feelings are to her at present so that we can compare them with her later emotions, after she has begun to "awaken."

Edna has always kept her distance from strong emotions. So far in this novel, she has been largely an observer. She is not sure how much of Robert's bravado she can believe. More important, however, she is sure that she is absolutely incapable of such intense feelings as her friends joke about, and she is even a little annoyed when Robert touches her casually while she is sketching a portrait of Adèle.

Chopin's tableau of this trio begins to close as Edna breaks off sketching for the day and fills the open hands of her children with bon-bons. Chopin tells us that "the sun was low in the west, and the breeze soft and languorous." Edna notices that Adèle, the ideal mother-woman, is a bit flushed; she wonders if Adèle's lively imagination is responsible. Edna is extremely curious about this mother-woman. As she did earlier, she watches this mother-woman as she greets her children, showering them with endearments. The mother-woman leaves, and Edna is left feeling free from the pressing duties of all of the Creole mother-women. For this reason, she is coaxed by Robert into taking an evening swim.

Chopin accompanies the scene with words that are very much like ones she used earlier: "The sun was low," she tells us, "and the breeze was soft and warm."

Chopin speaks of the sea and the sea's waves and the waves of wonder that Edna feels as she tries to fathom the mysterious Creole nature and as she tries to understand her feelings toward the sea. Edna is slowly awakening to the fact that the sea is beginning to speak to her, making her aware of its caressing quality and the embrace of its solitude. This will signal the dawn of one of several of Edna's "awakenings." Chopin describes the feeling on this particular night as "a certain light . . . beginning to dawn dimly with [Edna] – the light which, showing the way, forbids it." Edna is a stranger to the bewildering symptoms of troubled dreams, anguish, and uncontrolled sobbing, just as she is a stranger to the sensuous, delicious delight of feeling the sea fold around her body.

But Chopin does not leave us with merely metaphors. She wants her readers to clearly understand what her novel will deal with – the ecstasy and pain of sensuality and of romantic and sexual passion, subjects which were revolutionary in her time, especially for women writers. Chopin states clearly that Edna was "beginning to realize her position in the universe as a human being, and to recognize her relation as an individual to the world *within* and *about* her" (emphasis mine). She also makes it clear that Edna is not undergoing a mere, or brief, sudden, shadowy insight into life, or even vaguely sensing a simple lesson in maturity. Chopin will be challenging Edna with complex ideas and with "a ponderous weight of wisdom." At twenty-eight, Edna will receive "perhaps more wisdom than the Holy Ghost is usually pleased to vouchsafe to any woman." This is a strong comment; obviously men of the late nineteenth century granted little wisdom to women. But here Chopin accuses even God Himself of neglecting to grant women unusual wisdom. Edna, however, is to be an exception and, as Chopin's readers, we are curious and interested to see how Edna will receive and cope with this "ponderous weight of wisdom."

The voice of the sea ends the chapter. Chopin calls it "seductive; never ceasing, whispering, clamoring, murmuring; inviting the soul to wander for a spell in abysses of solitude; to lose itself in mazes of inward contemplation." This passage could have come directly from Walt Whitman's "Out of the Cradle Endlessly Rocking," a poem published some forty years before *The Awakening*. In his poem, Whitman speaks of the rocking rhythms of the sea, its powerful call, and its ability to "soothe, soothe, soothe!" Chopin, like Whitman, is aware that the sea invites the soul to wander, as it pulses with its sensual, caressing wetness. For Whitman, the sea was a symbol of rebirth. It will offer Edna a retreat, for awhile, away from life, an opportunity to rock her body and soul into a peace that will prelude her awakening so that she will emerge freshened, strengthened, and reborn.

When Robert asks her to accompany him for a swim, she declines, then reconsiders. Convention rather forbids it – swimming at evening time – yet Edna rather wants to swim, and so she accepts Robert's offer. After all, why not? Swimming, to Edna, is frankly sensuous, and its sensuality is enhanced by the handsome young man beside her. A healthy *man* would not hesitate to respond to the sea, and Edna is beginning to question why she, simply because she is a woman, should deny herself this gratification or why she should let society deny it to her. Edna, as we noted, is beginning "to recognize her relation as an individual to the world within and about her." She is aware that she is a separate, unique individual; she is *not* a mother-woman and, at twenty-eight, she is beginning to view herself in an entirely new perspective this summer as she lives among the Creole mother-women on Grand Isle.

Initially, Edna simply enjoyed swimming in the sea, but now something new is beginning to happen; her moments are no ordinary moments. Edna is allowing herself to become part of an unconscious fusion with the sea, feeling the echoes and the restless pull of the sea's waves within her body. In Edna's body, remember, there was a sea itself, one in which each of her children was rocked; the waves and the pull of this Gulf sea invite Edna back to it, just as it has invited generations of beings who left it long ago. The sea has always held a certain mystery and mystique; men have always been fascinated by it, but perhaps no man can fully feel the magic of it as a woman can. Edna cannot explain nor fathom the lure she feels. She only knows that she enjoys allowing herself to respond to it.

This is a moment of epiphany for Edna. She realizes innocently, without intellectually analyzing her feelings, that this seemingly quite ordinary moment – her deciding to swim in the sea and to freely enjoy her new emotional feelings about the sea – is more than a simple "swim." She is aware of the intense cleansing and renewing sense of this moment. Chopin applauds Edna's frankly sexual and spiritual response to the sea. She does not caution her readers against its seductive hold; on the contrary, she urges her readers to listen to the cadence of her prose as she attempts to evoke the feeling of this moment as Edna steps into the sea, succumbing to its strength as it speaks to her soul and to her body, "enfolding [her] in its soft, close embrace." Edna will soon be awakened to a new and fragile sexuality within herself. At the same time this happens, she will begin to sense within the sea the vast solitude that is within her and within humanity. Her awakening, then, will be double-edged: it will delight her and it will open new depths for her, and finally it will become her consolation.

CHAPTERS 7-10

After Chopin shows us Edna's mystical and sensuous immersion in the late evening sea, we witness Edna's relaxing her body and slowly releasing herself to new emotions and feelings. Then Chopin pulls back her narrative perspective and gives us some straightforward background exposition about the change that is to occur within Edna Pontellier. She tells us, for instance, that up to now Edna has always been a very private person, never given to confidences; even as a child, Edna had "her own small life all within herself." This small, private inner world, we realize, has continued to be characteristic of Edna throughout her adult life. She has whole dimensions of herself that she has not shared even with Léonce – nor with anyone else – until now. Now, a vague, undefined possibility of change occurring in her life has presented itself to Edna. This summer, she senses, will change the course of her life, and she is correct; neither she nor Léonce will ever be the same again.

At Grand Isle, she has allowed herself to be friendly with Robert – but only to a certain degree; it is therefore natural that she turns first to Adèle Ratignolle, another woman, when she feels the need to talk about herself. Adèle's unusual beauty so fascinates Edna that she believes that Adèle might perhaps be sympathetic to Edna's new, ambivalent feelings about discovering a new sense of beauty in living and, at the same time, a sense of confusion within herself.

As the two women walk along the beach, Chopin again contrasts them; their bodies seem parallels of their personalities. Adèle is "the more feminine and matronly"; Edna has "no suggestion of the trim, stereotyped fashion-plate . . ." Chopin adds that "a casual . . . observer . . . might not cast a second glance [at Edna]." Chopin is cautioning her readers not to label Edna as a stereotype who will be "awakened" in this novel and suddenly "bloom." Her "awakening" is far more important than a cliched, romantic, physical change. Edna is *not* the usual nineteenth-century heroine; Chopin stresses this point continually. She is, in Chopin's words, "different from the crowd."

In yet another of Chopin's tableaus, the two women are sitting by the sea, and its force and boundless freedom strengthens Edna's resolve to talk about herself. Symbolically, she removes her collar and "opens her dress at the throat" before she begins to speak. The lady in black is in the background, Chopin's ever-present symbol of death and danger, as are the two lovers, the antithetical symbols of a secure life and love.

Adèle instinctively senses that Edna needs to confess, and so she listens quietly as her friend reveals that sometimes as a young girl she could not resist reacting unexplainably to nature. One time, she remembers, she suddenly threw her arms outward, "swimming when she walked, beating the tall grass," and feeling as though she could walk on forever. She remembers that this was done on impulse. Usually she was not so spontaneous; she did not grow up that way. She grew up "driven by habit" and only now, this summer, have those feelings of childhood, those days when she wandered "idly, aimlessly, unthinking and unguided," returned to entice her. Adèle is clearly aware of how important this confession is to Edna and how different these new feelings are to her in contrast to her many years of living "by habit." Adèle is also aware that Edna does *not* withdraw her hand when Adèle covers it protectively; ordinarily, Edna avoids any sudden physical contact, as she did when Robert accidentally touched her while she was sketching. Adèle even strokes her friend's hand reassuringly, freely allowing her mother-woman instinct to comfort this woman who feels troubled here among the Creoles; she realizes that Edna feels unable to share in the Creole community of familiarities and is deeply confused by what is happening within her.

Chopin then removes us from this scene again; to help us understand Edna more fully (Edna will allow herself to tell Adèle only so much about her past), Chopin speaks directly to us. She tells us that Edna was not altogether comfortable with her young romantic feelings when she developed a schoolgirl crush on "a dignified and sad-eyed cavalry officer"; later, when her family moved from Kentucky to Mississippi, she developed a romantic crush on a young man, but the infatuation was brief and he was already engaged; as a grown woman, she fell in love with the face and figure and photograph of "a great tragedian." Her first romantic kisses were given to the cold glass that contained his photograph. It is no oversimplification: Edna has never known real love or real passion.

Chopin tells us frankly that Edna's marriage to Léonce Pontellier was "purely an accident." Léonce fell in love with Edna, he pressed for an answer, and Edna was flattered by his "absolute devotion." She imagined that there was "a sympathy of thought and taste between them." But despite the fact that there was no romance between herself and Léonce, Edna could *not* be convinced to reject this Creole Catholic man. She married Léonce despite the violent oppositions of both her father and her sister Margaret. Edna had been proposed to by a man who worshipped her, and if she married him, she felt that she would have a "certain dignity in the world of reality"; thus she consciously chose to close the door on a young woman's "realm of romance and dreams," and that door has remained closed until this summer when, by accident, she discovered it open, exposing old memories and old feelings, but more important, revealing fresh new concepts about herself and her emotional and physical needs.

Until now, Edna has been "fond" of Léonce; similarly, "in an uneven, impulsive way," she has been "fond" of her children. But nowhere does Chopin mention that Edna has a deep love for either Léonce or for the children. In fact, the months which her children spent with Léonce's mother granted Edna "a sort of relief." But, as was noted earlier, Edna cannot tell all of this to Adèle; she has lived too long encased in years of inner privacy. Of necessity, Chopin must tell this to us.

Talking so candidly with Adèle is almost traumatic for Edna, and Adèle understands this. She understands that Edna's sudden decision to confide in her has "muddled her like wine, or like a first breath of freedom." Edna is suddenly weak when Robert appears with "a troop of children," and she must gather up the loose ends of her thoughts, her reveries, and rearrange her composure. Adèle is keenly sensitive to the pain and confusion that has been laced throughout Edna's confessions, and it is for this reason that she feigns having such aching legs that Robert must assist her while they walk back to the cottage. She senses that Edna is beginning to fall in love for the first time, and she knows that she must warn Robert. Adèle and Robert have an old comradeship, and being old friends, they can seemingly discuss anything, and the mother-woman within Adèle is as protective of

Edna's tender new emotional awakenings as if Edna were one of Adèle's own children.

Adèle's request that Robert "let Mrs. Pontellier alone" is not received well. Robert realizes that his old friend is deadly serious, and he is momentarily disarmed; he is caught off-guard by Adèle's somber directness and, moreover, his pride is wounded when Adèle warns him that Edna "might make the unfortunate blunder of taking you seriously." Adèle's words sting because Robert has playfully toyed with married women for many summers, but until now he has not thought much about it; now Adèle has given Robert new insight into the emptiness of the "role" he has played and replayed in a long-running, trivial summer game. Before he leaves Adèle, Robert says with seriousness, softened by a smile, that she should not have warned him about Edna; rather, she should have warned him about himself, against *his* taking himself seriously. He leaves her then, and in the background are Chopin's familiar woman in black, looking even more ominously jaded, and the two lovers, seeming to be even more in love than ever. They are symbols, obviously, and are inserted here to prelude what is about to follow.

Robert's confusion, distraction, and irritation are apparent as soon as he enters his mother's house and hears the clacking noise of her sewing machine. Imaginatively, we can also hear the monotonous, mechanical clacking and parallel it with the monotonous, mechanical summer pattern that has been pivotal to Robert's summer years on Grand Isle. Yet it was a pattern which Robert enjoyed until Adèle made him realize how insignificant it was.

Robert inquires about the whereabouts of Mrs. Pontellier, and he reminds his mother that he promised to lend Edna the Goncourt. It is Robert now, not just Edna, who seems to be floundering. Ironically, Robert's life of simple spontaneity has been "driven by habit," just as Edna's life of bland sterility has been "driven by habit." And neither Robert nor Edna can fully understand nor grasp the changes that each of them instinctively feels is necessary for them. But Robert, however, seems far more alarmed and frantic than Edna, and when he remembers Adèle's capsule analysis of himself, it seems almost more than he can bear. It is easy to understand his thinking of Edna immediately; if no one takes him seriously, Adèle has said that Mrs. Pontellier might do so. The realization that he has been valued as no more than amusing summer entertainment is frightening to him. Like Edna, who is just beginning to discover how barren her life has been, Robert has suddenly viewed the deep void of his own life.

By accident that evening, he learns that Montel, an admirer of his mother, is in Vera Cruz, Mexico, and has inquired about Robert's joining him in a business venture. By chance, Robert suddenly realizes that two people, for the first time in years, are considering taking him seriously – Mrs. Pontellier and Montel. Mrs. Pontellier finds him romantic and Montel considers him mature enough to be a business partner. The temptation to suddenly prove himself and establish a sense of his own manhood is overwhelming. He chides his mother for not telling him sooner of Montel's offer, and he searches for the Goncourt to take to Mrs. Pontellier.

After Adèle warns Robert about the danger of Edna's susceptibility to his charms, Chopin allows a few weeks to pass. It is now Sunday and an impromptu party of sorts is underway; there is music, dancing, an unusual number of people, and even the children are allowed to stay up later than usual. The Farival twins who once irritated Léonce Pontellier with their piano playing are at the piano again, and even the parrot is once again shrieking outside the Lebrun doorway. Recitations are being given, as well as a performance by a young, amateur ballet dancer.

Edna joins the ballroom dancing for awhile, but soon prefers sitting outside on the gallery in the Gulf moonlight, watching the "mystic shimmer" on the "distant, restless water." Her revery is short-lived. Robert is determined to tempt her and please her, and he does so in a way that makes her the focus of the evening. Robert promises to have old Mademoiselle Reisz play the piano especially for Edna; he knows that he can charm the quarrelsome, eccentric old woman into performing, and he does. Entering the hall with Robert, Mademoiselle Reisz requests of Edna what music the lady would like to hear. Robert carries off his role of summer cavalier well, providing Edna with a gift of music and assuring himself that Adèle was right: Edna does take him seriously, and she is romantically fascinated by him; she is not like the Creole women with whom he played empty games during the past summers. Edna, of course, is ignorant of Robert's motives, and she is embarrassed and overwhelmed by what he does, and she begs that Mademoiselle Reisz choose suitable music. The old woman is intuitive about Robert's motives and about Edna's feelings toward Robert.

What Edna hears unnerves her. Chopin tells us that Edna has responded to piano music before, conjuring up vague moods of solitude, moods of longing and despair as embodiments of her own confused emotions, but Edna is totally unprepared for the raw passion that Mademoiselle Reisz sets ablaze within her, sending tremors down her spine, invading her soul and, sea-like, "swaying it, lashing it." Edna seems, we feel, almost ready to faint, feeling the music beating against her. She trembles and chokes, and tears blind her. Significantly, old Mademoiselle Reisz is aware of how successfully she has accomplished magic with her Slavic, romantic music.

Yet while Edna is the most visibly shaken, the entire company is moved by the music, and suddenly it is as though Robert "arranges" yet another bit of evening entertainment in yet another attempt to be taken seriously. Chopin tells us that Robert proposed that they all go for a swim "at that mystic hour under that mystic moon" and that "there was not a dissenting voice."

Robert is definitely assuming a new, commanding role in the novel, and while he does not "lead the way" to the beach, Chopin tells us that he "directed the way." Yet even he is not sure of the rules of his new role, for he finds himself "whether with malicious or mischievous intent" parting the two lovers that Chopin has included in various scenes and dividing them, as he walks between them.

Edna can hear Robert's voice from afar, but she is confused as to why he does not join her. She does not understand his new attitude. Once they were comfortable companions, and suddenly he has become unpredictable, absenting himself for a day, then redoubling what almost seems to be a kind of devotion to her the next day. It seems as though he is deliberately choosing to tease Edna, for Chopin tells us that Edna has begun to miss him, "just as one misses the sun on a cloudy day . . ." Clearly, Edna is falling in love with Robert, and he obviously is aware that she is doing so – becoming, in fact, seriously enamored of him. This is no longer the usual summer game of charade for him. Robert's attentions are being taken seriously by a monied, married woman, and he is enjoying his "seduction" of her; after all, he is a past master at such games.

It is now that we learn that Edna – all during the summer – despite all of her attempts, has never learned to actually swim. Despite her affection for the sea, she has never mastered it and while it lures her daily, it fills her with a "certain ungovernable dread." Tonight, however, all alone, she finds herself actually swimming for the first time in her life. The realization is overwhelming. Scarcely has she had time to adjust to Robert's generous attentions toward her than she was swept up by the power of Mademoiselle Reisz' romantic music, and now she discovers that she no longer has to "play" or "bathe" in the sea. Her emotions have been drained, yet she is giddy; she has gained a small bit of mastery—of herself and of the sea. It is almost as magical for her as Chopin has described the night as being.

Aware that she can actually swim gives Edna a new sense of freedom. She no longer needs a nearby hand. Her intoxication with her discovery makes her dramatically assertive; she wants to swim "where no woman had swum before," and she tries, swimming out alone, seaward, letting herself meet and melt with the pulsings she feels deep in the moonlit sea. Yet while she does not go any real distance, she goes far enough that she becomes frightened when she realizes that she might not be able to swim back. This is Edna's first encounter with the fear of death—yet another "awakening." But there is no one with whom she can share this terrible new discovery. Léonce is certainly not impressed that she can swim or that she is frightened. Not surprisingly, Edna chooses to leave him and return home alone. She is strongly affected by the rich magic of the music, by suddenly discovering the power of her swimming, and by the powerful fear that drowning is a possibility if one swims too far, alone.

Her senses are still swimming when Robert overtakes her; she is able to tell him, impulsively, exactly how she feels—of her exhaustion, of her joy, of her confusion, and of this night's being like a dream. She confesses that she feels possibly bewitched or enchanted.

Robert's response is dramatically on cue. He assumes the pose of a raconteur of Creole lore and interrupts her to explain that she has been singled out by a spirit that has "haunted these shores for ages." He fills Edna with romantic fancy, teasing her that perhaps the "spirit" that has found her may never release her. But he overplays his role; he gilds his fancy with too much embellishment, and Edna is finally hurt by his flippancy. Not being a Creole, she cannot respond with sufficient light wit and dash.

In the silence, Edna takes Robert's arm, then allows him to help her into a hammock. Both are aware that they are alone; she asks for her shawl, but she does not put it around her. Twice, Robert asks if he should stay until Mr. Pontellier returns and twice she says that he must decide. He smokes, they do not speak, yet she watches him, and in the silence, there are, Chopin tells us, "moments of silence . . . pregnant with the first felt throbbings of desire."

Robert leaves when the other bathers begin to approach, and when Edna says nothing, he believes that she is probably asleep. He could not be, ironically, more mistaken. Edna is fully awake, more awake than she has ever been in her life, aware of his body passing in and out of the strips of moonlight and, metaphorically, of his passing in and out of her body's desire for him.

Fittingly, Edna lies suspended in a hammock; she has learned to swim alone in the sea which she loves and which she now fears; she can almost joyously control this fierce natural power, yet she cannot wholly dominate it, for it fills her with a certain dread. Similarly, she has learned that her body has unloosened itself and she has let her emotions flow outward, unbounded; she has responded sexually to Robert's physical presence, yet, like the mysterious awe she has for the sea's power, she feels threatened by this new discovery of her sexuality because she cannot control what she does not understand. This night has engulfed her in multitudes of new emotions and discoveries. It is no accident that Chopin closes the chapter with Edna Pontellier suspended in a hammock, literally and symbolically suspended between a new reality and a night of magical awakenings.

CHAPTERS 11–14

It is a combination of exhilaration, a surge of new courage, a trace of fear, but most of all it is a sense of new peace that fills Edna Pontellier as she lies alone in her hammock. She does not even speak to Léonce when he returns home. In fact, she does not even answer him initially when he questions her, and note here how Chopin's style parallels Edna's inward transformation; in her narrative, Chopin tells us that Edna's eyes "gleamed," suggesting clear, direct sight and, further, Chopin says that Edna's eyes, despite the late hour, had "no sleepy shadows, as they looked into his." This descriptive phrase is doubly significant. It underscores Edna's newly awakened state, and it stresses Edna's looking directly at her husband, facing him as an equal and even as an opponent. Her voice rings with new authority as she tells him *no* – she is not asleep. Edna is absolutely awake and newly aware of her aroused physical feelings and emotions. Her "Don't wait for me" is symbolic of her new sense of life's enormous potential. Edna is no longer Léonce Pontellier's childlike lady-wife; she is no longer in need of a man's presence before she can begin readying herself for bed. She has awakened to a new confidence and to a new assertiveness within herself. Chopin emphasizes the seriousness of the metamorphosis that we are witnessing by telling us that ordinarily Edna would have obeyed her husband "through habit," would have "yielded . . . unthinkingly . . . [like] a daily treadmill of . . . life." Understandably, Léonce is puzzled by his wife's "whimsical" defiance, especially when she repeats once again that *no*, she is not going to bed; she is "going to stay out here."

At this point, one must turn backward toward a time long past and consider not only the courage it took for Edna to defy her husband, but also the courage it took for Chopin herself to envision such a scene as this and create the character of a "dutiful, submissive" wife suddenly asserting heretofore latent, unrealized willpower. For Léonce Pontellier, it must seem as though his wife is possessed and, to a degree, even Edna herself must feel a bit "possessed" as she realizes that "she could not at that moment have done other than denied and resisted" the force that she feels within her. The effect of Léonce's threat not to "permit" her to stay outside on the veranda is impotent, as is his derisive judgment that Edna's actions are more than "folly."

Léonce cannot comprehend the new voice he hears within his wife, a voice which has begun to articulate a new and independent identity. Heretofore, it has always been Léonce who has made all decisions, even minor ones. Now Edna has discovered the courage to hold her own nebulous future within her own two hands and, without rationally considering the consequences, she tells Léonce not to "speak to me like that again."

The silence is heavy. Léonce's preparations for bed are overly self-consciousness and nervous; he slips on "an extra garment," drinks two glasses of wine, and smokes several cigars. And all this time we are not even sure that Edna is conscious of her husband's puttering preparations for bed; she is experiencing a mildly chaotic ecstasy – "a delicious, grotesque, impossible dream." Truly, it must seem "grotesque" – Chopin's adjective is not too extravagant – for Edna Pontellier has come to the realization that it is *unnatural* for her to be dominated any longer by her husband. Chopin speaks of the "realities pressing into her soul" and of the "exuberance" exulting within her. Her words are suggestive of an intellectual, an emotional, and even a sexual climax within Edna; she has cut herself loose from the moorings of a life of attendance on monied, middle-class mores. Instead of stagnating in Léonce Pontellier's shallow marital confines, she has swum out and felt the cleansing power of new, fresh perceptions. She has never before sensed her own strength nor imagined that she could escape from an oppression which had always seemed a necessary dimension of a woman's lot.

After a few hours of feverish sleep, Edna's physical actions are not entirely strong. Chopin says that the cool morning air "steadied somewhat her faculties," but Chopin does not let her readers worry that Edna's "folly" (so termed by Léonce) was only momentary. Edna is as triumphantly awake in these morning hours as she was in the dark hours of the night and particularly this morning "she [is] not seeking refreshment or help from any source . . ." To describe Edna's new sense of herself, Chopin uses such words as "blindly following . . . alien hands . . . [which] freed her soul of responsibility."

This is a Sunday morning, and Chopin's Sabbath tableau includes once again the symbolic young lovers, strolling toward the wharf and also the lady in black. Edna, having passed through a night saying things to herself and to Léonce she has never said before, thinking things she has never thought before, and certainly doing things she has never done before, does something else this morning which she has never done before: she tells a little Negro girl who is sweeping the galleries to go and awaken Robert and tell him that she has decided to go to the Chênière, the nearby island where Sunday mass is held; moreover, Edna adds an afterthought of urgency: she says that the young girl should "tell him to hurry," and her impulsive decision to include an injunction to Robert contains three parallel phrases: "She had never . . . She had never . . . She had never . . ." All this must have seemed frighteningly revolutionary to women (and men) readers of 1899; revolt was a fearsome thing for those who had the abundance of leisure to read "novels," themselves things of "folly," according to many male intellectuals. Female independence was threatening; any modicum of liberty allowed to women was a dangerous risk. But Edna's defiance of her husband was clearly no whim that surfaced and disappeared during a night that Robert Lebrun mischievously termed as being "enchanted." Edna Pontellier is just as firmly assertive this morning as she was when she was lying in the hammock, and she is putting her new-found sense of liberty to a test. She commands Robert's presence, and he comes to her. Her future is dim and still vague, obscured by a present that is overpowering in its potential, but Edna is happy as she starts out on this small voyage to Sunday mass and on a much larger voyage out toward the fulfillment of her womanhood.

In addition to the collection of summer vacationers on the wharf, including the lovers and the lady in black, double-edged symbols of Edna's obscure new destiny as an independent woman, Chopin includes a new character in her Sunday tableau – a young Spanish girl, Mariequita. Mariequita is a pretty girl, and she and Robert speak Spanish briefly, a language that no one else understands. Edna notices the girl's feet: Mariequita is barefoot, her feet are broad, and there is "sand and slime between her brown toes." The girl is a flirt, openly "making 'eyes' at Robert," and tossing saucy comments to the man in charge of the boatload of passengers.

Although no one else understands what Robert and Mariequita are saying, Chopin reveals their conversation to us. Mariequita wants to know more about Robert's relationship with Edna; the fact that Edna is married is of no consequence to the young Spanish girl – marriage is no barrier to sexual satisfaction between two lovers, but she wants to know because she is interested in Robert herself: is Robert the lover of Mrs. Pontellier? Robert does not answer her directly; he teases and hushes her with a light jest. Meanwhile, Edna is dreamily intoxicated by the fierce new tenacity she feels within herself. As the boat's sails swell and become full-blown, Edna feels "borne away"; she feels "chains . . . loosening," and she feels "free to drift whithersoever *she* chose to set her sails" (emphasis mine). Her horizons are no longer limited. As the Sunday morning air strikes Edna's face, she is aware that she has been confined too long by social convention and marital muzzles.

Robert's spur-of-the-moment suggestion to Edna that they go to Grand Terre the next day excites Edna's new taste for boldness. She likes the idea of going and of being "alone there with Robert." Chopin stresses the physical satisfaction that Edna hopes will be hers when she imagines herself and Robert "in the sun, listening to the ocean roar and watching the slimy lizards writhe in and out among the ruins of the old fort." It is the seductive earthiness of the adventure that excites her, the pounding power of the ocean that fills her sense of adventure, and there is also a sexual suggestion when Chopin mentions the lizards writhing among the "ruins" of an old fort – symbolically, Edna's old fortress of middle-class security that she has been locked in until now. Neither Léonce nor even Robert fully comprehends this new woman; Robert asks if Edna won't be afraid of crossing the sea in a canoe, and Edna's "no " is sure and assertive. This causes Robert to promise her other trips, at night; then he slips into his jester's role, teasing her again about the "Gulf spirit" and warning her that it will whisper to her where hidden treasures can be found. Spontaneously, Edna matches Robert's imaginative caprices, saying extravagantly that she will squander any pirate gold they might find and throw it to the four winds, just "for the fun of seeing the golden specks fly." Edna is rich already; she has unearthed her own hidden treasure – herself, and the sureness of herself; it is exciting to see her laughing so freely and fancifully about imaginary hidden treasures.

Significantly, the oppressiveness of the church service becomes so restrictive and stifling that Edna is forced to leave the service. The ritual of the circumscribed dogma filling the tiny enclosure begins to suffocate Edna's new, bursting spirit. To be imprisoned so soon after she has experienced a breath of freedom is impossible for her. Robert solicitiously follows her out of the church and instinctively, perhaps, takes her where she can hear "the voice of the sea." She takes a drink from a rusty cistern and is "greatly revived"; this is Chopin's symbolic mass for Edna – a baptism with water that is holy not because it is divinely sanctified but because it comes from the earth and is naturally cool and refreshing to Edna's *physical* body, as well as to her spiritual body.

At Madame Antoine's, where Robert takes Edna, notice the freedom which Edna feels when she decides to loosen and remove her clothes, how responsive she is to the feel of the sheets and to the odor of laurel in the air; there is a sensuousness within her as she stretches her body to its full length. Edna is discovering the pleasure of physical self-awareness, how delicious her own body can feel. This is part of the "ponderous weight of wisdom" that Chopin spoke of earlier. Edna is claiming, as well as discovering, her own sensuality: "she saw for the first time, the fine, firm quality and texture of her flesh."

After she sleeps long and soundly and awakens late in the afternoon, her first words to Robert strike him as somewhat fey, but they are symbolically full of great significance: "How many years have I slept?" Robert's playful joking about her sleeping one hundred years seems romantically the right kind of response from this young man who has, summer after summer, assumed the role of a knight errant, attending some fair lady at his mother's summer resort. But Edna's question, if exaggerated, is weighty. She has metaphorically been asleep a very long time. And as she awakens from her late afternoon nap, she is also just beginning to awaken to the reality of an identity crisis. Of course, at this moment it is no crisis – that will come later – but the immediacy of her new identity is of concern and that concern now is with her resolve to commit herself fully to the new identity that she conceives is possible for her – whatever that illusive, unformed, unimaginable identity might be.

Among Edna's many thoughts, she considers whether or not Léonce will be "uneasy," but note that this is only a "consideration" for her; it is not a concern that he might be worried about her. We must realize that Edna no longer fears a possible reproach from him for her "folly," as Léonce will no doubt declare her actions to be.

When Robert and Edna sit down to eat at Madame Antoine's, Robert notices the "relish" with which Edna eats; she is discovering new and satisfying sensations in even such commonplace acts as eating. Her appetite for food and, more important, her appetite for living has been whetted and sharpened. She allows herself the freedom to sit under the orange trees, watch the shadows lengthen, and listen to the Creole tales and fancies of Madame Antoine until "the night came on." She is severing herself, freeing herself to absorb what is offered to her – the food, the cooling air from the sea, and the compelling, storytelling voice of Madame Antoine. These moments are not dictated by "habit" or directed by a mindless adherence to duty or by any other consideration, save one: herself. Feeling freed from a past of repression, Edna allows herself to linger fully in the luxuriousness of this moment.

This long Sunday afternoon has not been satisfying for the rest of Edna's family. Adèle Ratignolle, however, Edna's mother-woman confidante, has been able to coddle and pacify the younger of Edna's children, as well as Edna's husband, who has gone off to discuss the latest happenings of the cotton exchange. Now that Edna has returned, Adèle admits to suffering from the heat, and she refuses to remain even for a moment with her friend, even to hear about Edna's after-noon adventures. Monsieur Ratignolle is "alone, and he detested above all things to be left alone." The contrast between Edna's new sense of herself and her role as a wife and mother is in bold contrast to Adèle's life, governed wholly by domestic duties and demands; she must take charge of and take care of a multitude of mother-woman things – food, children, and a husband. She satisfies herself by being useful to them; she knows of no other possible pleasure for herself. Her value lies in her devotion to her utility – to the man she married and to their children.

When Robert leaves Edna finally, after both children are in bed, Edna asks him with the wonder of a child who realizes that some-thing very special has happened, if *he* realizes that they have been together "the whole livelong day." His answer is serious, despite his surface joking: "all but the hundred years when you were sleeping," and when he leaves, Chopin tells us that he goes not to join the others, but that he walks alone toward the Gulf. This afternoon has touched Robert also.

Alone, Edna breathes deeply and her sense of solitude swells; she allows her mind to billow backward over the long day's length, try-ing to discover "wherein" this summer has become suddenly different from "every other summer of her life." Softly, she sings a song to her-self that Robert sang earlier, the refrain returning after each verse, "*si tu savais*": "if you only knew . . ." There is little doubt that she is falling in love with her fresh sense of freedom, in love with the sense of adventure she has discovered in life and in herself, and in love with Robert.

CHAPTERS 15–16

Time passes – we cannot be sure how long – and Chopin begins this chapter with startling news: Edna comes to dinner and is told simultaneously by several guests that Robert has decided to go to Mexico. What has happened between the two of them since we left them on that Sunday evening and this moment we can measure only by Edna's genuine confusion. For example, they spent the entire morn-ing together, and Robert did not mention Mexico. His leaving Grand Isle so rashly seems unreal, and as Edna sits across from him at dinner, she allows him – and everyone else – to see her undisguised bewilder-

38

ment. Robert looks both embarrassed and uneasy when Edna asks "of everybody in general" when he is going. When she learns that he intends to leave this very evening, her voice rises in astonishment at the utter impossibility of such an unexpected exodus. Even Robert's voice begins to rise, Chopin tells us, as he defensively explains that he has said "all along" that he was going to Mexico. Only the two high-pitched voices are haranguing, and yet Madame Lebrun must finally knock on the table with her knife handle and declare that her table is becoming a bedlam.

It is an awkward scene as Robert is forced to admit that his decision was made only this afternoon. As he explains his actions to Edna, Chopin describes him as feeling as though he is "defending himself against a swarm of stinging insects"; explaining his leaving to the other guests, Robert is characterized as feeling like a "criminal in a court of justice." Edna senses that his answers are too lofty and that he is posturing; we feel this too. It is as though Robert is trying to make his decision to go to Mexico seem like a mature decision made after long months of weighing and mulling over the alternatives and advantages—instead of the hasty escape from Grand Isle that Edna half-fears and half-believes that it may be.

Later, Adèle Ratignolle's mother-woman instincts try to comfort Edna; what Adèle feared at the beginning of the summer has happened: Edna has fallen in love with Robert Lebrun. Adèle assures Edna that Robert was wrong to say nothing about his leaving until only moments before he was due to leave, but she thinks that Edna should, for manners' sake, join her and the others in seeing Robert off; otherwise, it won't "look friendly." Here, she reveals how thoroughly imprisoned and confined she is in her prescribed role as a perfect and proper mother, wife, and woman. Adèle cautions Edna not to expose her emotions, especially her wounded feelings toward Robert; even if Edna's heart is broken, she should camouflage her shattered dreams and submissively join the rest of the guests. Edna's pride, however, refuses to yield to her friend's pleadings, and it is Robert who finally seeks out Edna, instead of the traditional frantic female pursuing the departing male.

Bluntly, Edna asks Robert how long he will be gone; she admits that she is unhappy and doesn't understand him or his silence. Edna plays no games. Her love for Robert has no coy edges; she admits to having daydreamed of seeing him often in New Orleans after the summer was over. Robert half-confesses to having had the same hopes, then breaks off, assuming the manners of a gentleman, extending his hand, and addressing her as "Mrs. Pontellier." Edna cannot, or will not, conceal her hurt and disappointment; clinging to his hand, she asks him to at least write to her, and he promises to do so. Then he is gone. Edna struggles to keep from crying, from lapsing into silly, adolescent feelings of desertion. She realizes all too well what has happened; she allowed herself to take Robert's presence for granted, just as she allowed herself to joyously take for granted her newly discovered feelings of independence and the knowledge that she was in love with young Robert Lebrun. There is, however, nothing to be done now. Robert will be gone in a few minutes.

Edna's suffering and pain in this scene is another of her awakenings; when she opened herself to the possibility of passion for a man, she should also have included the possibility of great pain. It seems a simple enough equation, but Edna was still a naive woman, even though she was twenty eight years old when she fell in love for the first time. Yet once she accepted the profound delights of love, she should also have realized the possibility of profound pain as being the probable denouement of love between a married woman and a single man in the restricted, patriarchal southern society of 1899. Edna, however, is an innocent and she committed emotional adultery without forethought and without guilt because of her loveless marriage.

In contrast, Robert—a role-oriented and role-defined Creole—cannot break his community's mores. We sense that he has fallen in love with Edna, but that he is unwilling to risk an affair with her—out of respect for her and out of respect for a code which forbids it. Thus he flees to Mexico rather than confront his feelings for her; he refuses to resolve or cope with what seems to be an unsolvable dilemma. Throughout this summer, he has been Edna's teacher; he opened her soul to spiritual and physical delights, but when he realized that he was falling in love with his married, adoring pupil, he could not deal with his desire for her. His long-time fantasy of going to Mexico and finding success and happiness abruptly became an instantaneous destination for him. To remain in Grand Isle and become Edna's lover would make him a cad; to exit to Mexico is the way of a coward, yet he sees no alternative for himself. He is too weak to stay, and his weakness accentuates Edna's emotional heroism.

Seemingly, she would be willing to risk everything; Robert cannot commit himself to such a decision.

After Robert's departure, Chopin tells us that Edna spent much time in a "diversion which afforded her the only pleasurable moments she knew"—that is, swimming in the sea. Edna belongs to no "community" here, in the way that Adèle belongs to her community of mother-women. Without Robert's companionship, Edna feels her closest kinship with the sea, especially now that she has learned to swim. Remember that the sea once offered her the soothing company of its solitude. Now she returns to it.

The Creole community misses Robert's vivacious presence; they naturally assume that Edna does also. Certainly Léonce is aware that his wife greatly misses her young friend. Yet no one guesses the extent to which Edna is pained by Robert's absence. Chopin speaks of Edna's unconsciously looking for him, seeking out others to talk about him, and gazing at old photographs of Robert in Madame Lebrun's sewing room, taken when he was a young boy. One photograph in particular amuses her—a picture of Robert, looking "full of fire, ambition and great intentions." It is a positive sign of Edna's growing maturity that she is able to smile at that picture. Despite her pain of missing him, she knows full well that she is infatuated with a man who is sorely lacking "fire, ambition and great intentions." Robert is, by nature, gentle, sensuous, and a dreamer; it was these qualities that first attracted Edna to him. And because he is basically a gentle young man, his abrupt severing of their relationship is all the more painful.

We now encounter a passage in the novel that probably shocked Chopin's readers far more than the notion of Edna's romantic need for an "affair." We learn that Edna and Adèle Ratignolle once had a rather heated argument during which Edna told her mother-woman confidante that she "would give [up her] money, I would give my life for my children, but I wouldn't give myself"—that is, Edna would *not* sacrifice day after day of living an empty, unfulfilled life for her children's sake—"or for anyone." She would, if ever such a drastic choice were necessary, sacrifice her life so that her children might live, but she would *never* live an empty life, devoted solely to her children, dedicated to them, doing everything for *their* sakes. She could never define herself in terms of them, nor would she use their lives as a surrogate for her own life.

Surely this was the fullest declaration of independence uttered by a heroine in a novel that Chopin's readers had ever encountered. Many novels prior to *The Awakening* had contained episodes in which married heroines left their husbands for another man, or had an affair with a young lover, but here was a woman who defied the whole concept of the family unit. Edna would give her life, if necessary, for her children, but she would not live an empty life dedicated to anyone – save herself and what *she* considered essential for herself. This is as shockingly revolutionary to Adèle Ratignolle as it must have been to Chopin's readers and early critics. The whole masculine-conceived, family-oriented universe is being suddenly defied by young Edna Pontellier. Edna is protesting against a woman's living vicariously through the lives of her husband, her children, or anyone else. Edna demands full responsibility for herself – and to herself. She refuses to dedicate her life to a role that she does not fashion, define, and fulfill.

CHAPTERS 17–19

Within two weeks, the Pontelliers are reestablished in their large house in New Orleans. Seemingly, they are the happy master and mistress of the charming, many-columned, broad verandaed home, and Chopin details for us its dazzling white exterior, contrasting it with the serenity of the inner furnishings – the soft carpets, the damask draperies, the cut glass, the silver, and the rich paintings – all presents from Mr. Pontellier to Edna, "the envy of many women whose husbands were less generous than Mr. Pontellier." Mr. Pontellier takes great pride while walking through his house, surveying its sumptuous details. "He greatly valued his possessions," Chopin states, and we recall a sentence near the beginning of the novel when he irritably commented on his wife's sun-bronzed body. He scolded that she was "burnt beyond recognition . . . looking at his wife as one looks at a valuable piece of personal property which has suffered some damage." Léonce Pontellier esteems "his possessions, chiefly because they [are] *his*" (emphasis mine). Among his possessions, he obviously and unthinkingly includes his wife because he lives in an era when he and his men friends conceive of their wives in terms of their being personal possessions.

The lazy summer days of the Gulf resort seem remote as Chopin describes the Tuesdays which are Edna's official "reception days," when "a constant stream" (an ironic image here) of lady callers alight from carriages or stoll up to the front door, greet the mulatto houseboy, who holds a tiny silver tray for their calling cards, and are offered liqueur, coffee, or chocolate before they are finally allowed to greet the mistress of this elegant mansion: "Mrs. Léonce Pontellier, attired in a handsome reception gown." This role has occupied and embodied Edna's existence ever since she became Mrs. Pontellier, six years ago. Certain evenings are designated for the opera, and others are for plays; days are scheduled very much alike – Mr. Pontellier leaving between nine and ten o'clock and returning between six and seven in the evenings, and dinner is always at half past seven.

It is on one of these Tuesdays when Léonce returns home and notices, much as he might detect an unexpected crack in an expensive china bowl, that his wife is not wearing a reception gown; she is wearing an ordinary housedress. Léonce comments that no doubt she is overly tired after her many callers, and Edna confirms that there were indeed many callers – at least there were many cards in the silver tray when she returned. Deliberately, she does not say from where she had returned. Edna has broken a long-established pattern: she was not a "hostess" today.

Léonce is almost, but not quite, angry with her. He is busy adding condiments to his soup, scolding her softly: "people don't do such things" – unless they have a good excuse. Edna has no excuse, nor did she leave any explanation for her callers, nor does she offer any to Léonce.

Mr. Pontellier explains to his wife, much as he would to an absent-minded maid or a socially backward daughter, that they both must observe "*les convenances*" (the conventions). That his chiding is done in French is an added affront of smug male superiority, as is his cranky complaining about the tastelessness of the soup, as though he were a culinary authority. He requests that the silver tray of cards be brought to him; social callers musn't be snubbed – especially the monied ones, he comments, as he discovers that a certain Mrs. Belthrop found his wife not at home this afternoon. He tries to humor Edna and make her realize that these niceties *are* important, and he insists that she must apologize to a certain caller and that she must avoid another. Just as he has *his* business duties, Edna has *her* social duties, which are an important extension of his business world.

Mr. Pontellier's critical evaluations continue and include each of the food courses, all of which he finds fault with. "Cooks are only human," he says, implying that hired help must be constantly kept on guard lest they become lazy. He adds that hired help, if not watched carefully, will soon "run things their own way." The phrase is intense with significance. Mrs. Pontellier's refusing to perform the social pattern of her Tuesdays, as she has for six years, is an example of someone deciding to do "things their own way." And while Edna cannot literally be considered an employee of Mr. Pontellier, he certainly considers her a functionary in the house. His comment is purposely pointed. Of course, he rewards Edna generously for performing her duties, but that means that she is duty-bound to repeat on each Tuesday a succession of mindless greetings and chatter to insure and further the Pontelliers' social status. Edna is symbolically and, in fact, a costly, performing puppetlike possession of Mr. Pontellier. Their marriage ceremony decreed it, he identifies her as such, and he expects *her* to do likewise. As a reward, he bestows every possible material thing of value upon her so that she will further enhance him and be satisfied with being defined as "Mrs. Léonce Pontellier." She is envied. He knows it, and other people know it, and being envied is of much importance to Mr. Pontellier.

There were times, Chopin tells us, when Edna attempted to plan a menu or when she studied cookbooks, trying to please her husband's highly critical expectations, but those days are over. Tonight, after Edna finishes dinner, she goes to her room and stands in front of an open window. At this point in the novel, one can't even imagine Edna's standing in front of a *closed* window; she has finally felt the satisfaction of independent judgments and actions, and the open window is symbolic of the free flowing, fresh air of freedom. Edna is not terribly unhappy tonight; she is frustrated. She recognizes the mystery of the night beyond the window. It revives old memories, but she is not soothed by them. She paces, she tears a tiny handkerchief to ribbons, then flings her wedding ring onto the carpet, and stamps the heel of her shoe upon it as though she could crush it. The strength of the tiny gold band, however, mocks her frustration and causes her to grab up a glass vase and fling it onto the tiles of the hearth. The crash and clatter are welcome sounds of destruction – until a well-trained maid hurries in and begins cleaning up the mess. When the maid returns the ring to Edna, she slips it on, slipping uncomfortably once again into the tightly restricted role of being Mrs. Léonce Pontellier.

The following morning, the Pontelliers quarrel briefly about new fixtures for the library. Edna thinks that her husband is excessively extravagant for wanting to buy them; he regrets that she doesn't feel like selecting them. Cautioning her to rest and take care of herself, he takes his leave and Edna is left alone. The world beyond the Pontellier veranda is fragrant with flowers and noisy with street vendors and young children. Edna, however, feels alienated from them, alienated from everything and everyone around her. Chopin has built up a good deal of tension and suspense. Edna is about to do something. Her frustration will not allow her to return to a world where she ignorantly and innocently half-lived for six years as her husband's charming hostess and wife and the dutiful mother of his children.

Edna leaves the house, and as she walks we learn that "she [is] still under the spell of her infatuation." She has tried to forget Robert, but has been unsuccessful. As she did on Grand Isle, Edna has decided to seek out Adèle Ratignolle and try to talk about her problems. The two women are confidantes, even though the Ratignolles are certainly less well off, materially and socially, than the Pontelliers. They live above their drug store, prosperous though its trade is, in an apartment, commodious though it might be. Adèle does not have a "receiving day"; she has, instead, once every two weeks, *soirees musicales*, evenings of musical entertainment which are very popular and considered a privilege to be invited to.

The mother-woman is unsurprisingly busy, sorting the family laundry; she says that it is really the maid's work, but she enjoys doing it, yet stops to chat with Edna. Once again, Chopin contrasts the two women. The domestic harmony that Edna sees is pleasing but she does not and cannot belong to that world. Edna can never find full, true contentment folding laundry, preparing meals, and listening with honest interest to her husband's dinner talk. That world is colorless, boring, and confining to Edna. It contains no measure of exhilaration and nothing of what Edna suddenly voices in her inner thoughts as "the taste of life's delirium." Chopin comments that "Edna vaguely wondered what she meant by 'life's delirium.' "

Chopin's readers were also probably puzzled by that phrase. Modern readers, however, do not find the term puzzling at all; it seems antiquated in its articulation perhaps, but we do not "vaguely wonder" about the meaning of the term. We realize that Edna is beginning to demand for herself no more or no less than the right to experience the fullness of her emotional spectrum. The solidarity of the Ratignolles' lifestyle is too mechanical and unimaginative; it is constructed on routine and precludes all possibility of unbounded pleasure and passion, as well as violent pain. Edna finds no consolation in Adèle's maternal security and happiness. Adèle has traded her identity and her independence for serenity and security. Adèle's life is centered on her utilitarianism, just as Léonce's world is centered on material possessions and social position. A free existence for a woman—devoid of her being equated with husband, children, and household chores—was unheard of in 1899, unless one were an "artist." And this seems to be at least a possibility for Edna. She lives in New Orleans, a city filled with writers, painters, and artistic types; Edna is beginning to envision that perhaps this lifestyle is her only alternative. The position of being sovereign of the Pontellier mansion that Léonce offers to her is repugnant. Léonce places Edna on a pedestal, yet at the same time he shackles her there. Edna wants to break these chains. It is a dangerous, nebulous ideal that Edna desires; years later, a modern Greek writer, Nikos Kazantsakis, articulated precisely the yearnings of this frustrated Victorian woman in his novel *Zorba the Greek*. The hero, speaking to a rather prudish young Englishman, tells his friend that one "must, sometimes, cut the rope [of rationality]; a man needs a little madness in his life." Zorba, of course, would (like Léonce Pontellier) deny such freedom to a woman. But not Chopin. She created a heroine who, like Zorba, wanted "a little madness" in her life, something besides the dull and conventional and stifling role that was forced on her by generations of men and by their submissive wives, as well. Edna is beginning to distrust the value of permanence and is beginning to trust the value of her instincts. She was awakened on Grand Isle to feel that there was a possiblity for her to be more than a wife and more than a mother; she is not sure *what*, but she is certain of the possibility.

Unfortunately, Léonce Pontellier is not aware of this change within his wife. He expected her to begin once again the patterned ritual of their New Orleans social life once they returned to the city for the winter. Edna cannot; she is struggling with her deliverance from that role, and she feels within her a force superior to Léonce's drive for power and position and also superior to Adèle's happy security within the four walls of Monsieur Ratignolle's home.

It was childish to stamp on her wedding ring; it was childish to smash a vase. Edna realizes that she was acting exactly like a frustrated child. Yet Léonce conceives of his wife as childlike; he assumes that she will accept docility and dependence as her natural lot. Ironically, she behaved exactly like Léonce's child-wife, the person whom she desperately tries *not* to be. And in order "to do as she liked and to *feel* as she liked" (emphasis mine), Edna realizes that she must control her emotions, as well as her actions. As long as she is smashing vases and raging, she is denying herself moments of self-declared and self-defined control. She can complain as loudly as she wishes, but unless she begins to act upon her own convictions, she will be doomed to the futile, cliched role of being yet another woman moaning about the injustice of the world and blaming men for her misery. Her violence was spontaneous, but it ultimately solved nothing. It left her as powerless as before. But she will *not* be bought or compromised by the promise of new library furnishings or the threats of social disapproval.

Thus Edna decides to completely abandon her "Tuesdays at home"—an act of social revolution that was unheard of in the Pontelliers' New Orleans social circle. Nor does Edna explain her decision—just as she refuses to return the visits of her lady callers.

Mr. Pontellier is at first bewildered, then shocked, and is finally angered that his wife means to exchange the role of being "head of a household" for being a painter in an atelier. Her lack of logic confuses him, but it does not confuse or even frighten Edna. For the moment, she *feels* like painting; "perhaps I shan't always feel like it," she says, knowing and admitting to Léonce that she is "not a painter." She does not know *why* she is doing what she is doing, but it is what she *must* do. Edna is hearing and responding to the beat of what Thoreau calls "a different drummer," and she is following it without being overly concerned about her final destination. A man in her time could have been able to do the same thing and no one would have questioned his gambling with life. Nor would they have been shocked by his admission that his ultimate goals were undefined; after all, Robert was able to pack up and suddenly leave for Mexico, and the only consternation concerned his sudden departure—not his actual leaving. Such things are possible—if one is a man. Edna wants that same choice for herself; it is her only hope of release from years of habitual submission.

When she was on Grand Isle, swimming in the sea, listening to its soothing music of freedom, feeling it surround her – all this intoxicated her. It relieved her from the heavy weight of nineteenth-century New Orleans convention. Her exultation unlocked her; Edna is shedding a fictional self that Léonce and even she herself created for her, dressed her in, and taught her to perform as.

Léonce allows her this "whim"; like a restless child, his wife will tire of dabbling in painting and dawdling in obscure, transient "folly"; he is sure of this. He could not be more mistaken. Edna knows that she is no great painter; she never intends to turn out great masterpieces of art. She simply needs to paint at the present and, most important, she needs *not* to entertain boring streams of women callers every Tuesday.

Edna works, then, with great energy – "without accomplishing anything" – but as she draws and paints, she sings to herself the refrain that Robert sang after they had spent the day on the island of Chênière Caminada. The memory of the rippling water and the flapping sails are sensual memories, preludes to her body's remembering "a subtle current of desire." This is not simple romantic revery; this is richly sexual, a yearning to have the desire consummated. Chopin is boldly stating that a woman experiences the same sexual excitement and needs that a man does when she is aroused by certain smells and certain sounds and memories. The memories of the brief hours spent with Robert exude the heat of an aphrodisiac for Edna, a concept considered unhealthy and akin to heresy in Chopin's time.

Edna's desires must, of necessity, remain unsatisfied, but she accepts the inevitable – for the present. She knows that she can recreate and rekindle the fire within herself, even if she cannot satisfy it. This is part of the breadth of the emotional spectrum that Edna claims for herself in exchange for her former role as wife and possession of the well-to-do Léonce Pontellier.

CHAPTERS 20–24

Although Edna is not completely satisfied with being an "artist," she continues to paint; being a painter frees her to a great extent, and it causes her to seek out another woman who is also an artist, a character from the past—old Mademoiselle Reisz, the pianist who played the powerfully passionate music the night Edna discovered that she could actually swim; it was also on that night that she discovered the courage to defy her husband's demands that she obey something as insignificant as "coming to bed" because of the possibility of being "devoured by mosquitoes." Edna cannot easily locate the old woman's address, but her impetuous decision to find the old woman becomes a challenge for Edna. She follows suggestions from strangers, is led to new neighborhoods, hears disagreeable gossip from those who claim to have known her, but Mademoiselle Reisz herself remains illusive until Edna remembers that if anyone would know the whereabouts of the eccentric musician, it would probably be her summer landlady, Madame Lebrun, now living in New Orleans for the winter months.

Ironically, it is while Edna is on this capricious, independent adventure that she hears a quarrel within the Lebrun house before the door is opened. A black servant is demanding of Victor, Robert's brother, that *she* be allowed to open the door; it is her duty. This is sharply symbolic. Chopin is contrasting Edna's new independence with the actions of a servile, submissive black servant; it is inserted inobtrusively, yet very naturally, into the scene, as Chopin quietly denounces pride in what is ultimately an abject role.

It is Victor, Robert's handsome, nineteen-year-old brother, who greets Edna with undisguised delight, and he allows Edna to sit on the side porch instead of "properly" guiding her into the parlor. Impetuously, he begins to tell the handsome older woman about a romantic escapade he had the night before when he followed the flirtatious lead of a girl who was taken by his good looks. This is obviously something he would never tell his mother, but he feels—after the summer that he observed Edna on Grand Isle—that Edna is "different," even if she is older than he is, and a wife and a mother.

Edna indulges Victor's imaginative, male bravado-embroidered storytelling until Madame Lebrun enters. The family, she learns, has received two letters from Robert, letters which Victor declares to be of little value and glibly recites the contents of. Futilely, of course, Edna had hoped for some greeting to her; instead, Robert simply asked that his mother remember him affectionately to "all his friends."

Edna's mood darkens briefly, but because the Lebruns know old Mademoiselle Reisz' address, Edna leaves the Lebrun house in good spirits. Not only Madame Lebrun notices how "handsome" Edna looks, but Edna's beauty has not escaped Victor; "ravishing" is how he describes her, commenting that ". . . she doesn't seem like the same woman."

Mademoiselle Reisz also comments on Edna's handsome, healthy looks. She prides herself on a candor that she can afford because of her old age and "artistic" eccentricity. Edna, however, is also direct — because she *chooses* to be. When the old pianist says that she feared that Edna would not come to see her in New Orleans, she is told candidly that Edna herself has not been sure whether or not she likes the woman — a frankness that pleases the old woman. She therefore quickly reveals the fact that she has had a letter from Robert, written in Mexico City. But she refuses to let Edna read the letter, even though she says that it contains nothing but questions about, and recollections of, Edna. In particular, Robert asks Mademoiselle Reisz to play the Polish composer Chopin's "Impromptu" for Edna, should Edna pay a call on Mademoiselle Reisz. According to Mademoiselle Reisz, Robert wants to know, afterward, how the music affects Edna.

The old woman is teasing Edna. We sense that she is trying to measure Edna's passion for young Robert, trying to determine whether or not Edna is merely a dilettantish, frivolous, bored wife of the well-to-do Mr. Pontellier. She is trying to decide whether or not Edna is merely dabbling in painting and pretending passion for a young man who is living in an exotic, faraway country. Therefore, she does not play merely the Chopin "Impromptu"; she combines it with one of Wagner's love themes, hoping that her background mood music will expose the truth of Edna's emotions as she reads Robert's letter. The music, the deep shadows in the little room, the night air, and Mademoiselle Reisz' music all cause Edna to begin sobbing — something she has not done since a night long ago on Grand Isle.

Léonce Pontellier decides to call up his old friend Doctor Mandelet, a "semiretired physician . . . [who has] a reputation for wisdom rather than skill," and it must have given Chopin much secret delight to write an entire chapter, short though it is, devoted to "man talk" about women. Mr. Pontellier boasts of his own manly good health and his healthy Creole genes — in contrast to his wife who, while not sick, is "not like herself." The two men agree that women are moody, delicate creatures, not to be fully understood. Of course, however, Mr. Pontellier assures the old doctor that Edna's *heredity* has nothing to do with her problems. He *chose* her from "sound old Presbyterian Kentucky stock"; Chopin's satire is especially keen here. In particular, Mr. Pontellier is puzzled about Edna's notions that she has recently acquired "concerning the eternal rights of women." This also causes the old doctor some concern as he lifts "his shaggy eyebrows," protrudes "his thick nether lip," and taps "the arms of his chair . . ." Chopin's portrait is magnificent. Léonce continues: Edna isn't interested in attending her younger sister's wedding; she says that "a wedding is one of the most lamentable spectacles on earth." The doctor nods; Edna is another woman "going through a phase." He assures Mr. Pontellier that "the mood will pass . . . it will pass; have patience." Secretly, the old doctor wonders if another man might be involved in Edna's personality change, but he knows better than insult Mr. Pontellier with such a question.

The introduction of Edna's father into the narrative is unexpected; he was mentioned at the beginning of the novel, when we learned that he had once owned a Mississippi plantation before he settled in the bluegrass country of Kentucky, and we recall that he was not merely opposed to Edna's marriage to Léonce, a Catholic Creole, but that he was "violently opposed." Edna is "not warmly or deeply attached" to her father, but most of their antagonism seems to have faded; she welcomes his coming to New Orleans as a distraction from her own indecision about what she must ultimately do with her life.

Adèle Ratignolle, Edna's confidante, urges Edna to encourage Léonce to spend more time at home and less time at his men's club. Edna does not understand how this would solve anything; "What should I do if he stayed home? We wouldn't have anything to say to each other," she counters. And frequently while reading this novel, one needs to go back almost a century and imagine the readers of this novel and the critics who were suddenly confronted with such intimate, honest declarations as this. It is little wonder that they were puzzled, shocked, and offended. Yet Chopin is not being racy. She is simply allowing Edna to speak openly about the emptiness of her marriage. Almost a hundred years later, the problems of such marital voids are the subject of many monthly articles in magazines in the supermarkets and drugstores, but in Chopin's day, such indiscretions were considered, if not sinful, at least a defect on the part of a negligent, willful wife. It was a wife's duty to keep her marriage harmonious—at any cost—sincerely, as well as superficially. Edna will not permit any of this mindless convention, especially now that she realizes what thoroughly different people she and Léonce are. Her moments of anguish may be painful, but she plumbs them and exhausts them, and she does not harbor them morbidly or roman- tically. And when they are finished, she opens herself to new experi- ences, just as she does in this chapter when she and her father share rare moments of excitement and thrills at the racetrack. Doctor Mandelet is particularly struck by Edna's radiance when he sees her; there is none of the mysterious moodiness that Léonce was worried about. Yet the old doctor is not pleased to learn that Edna encountered Alcée Arobin, a man we heard about earlier, in Chapter 8, when tongues clucked about his affair with the consul's wife at Biloxi. The old doctor fears that a rich (and bored – if Léonce's assessment can be relied on) wife might be an easy target for the notorious heart- breaker; in addition, the doctor notices that Edna has a new "animal" vitality; Léonce Pontellier's wife seems "palpitant with the forces of life . . . [like] some beautiful sleek animal waking up in the sun" – an even more dangerous ingredient in the possibility that she and Arobin find one another attractive, fascinating, and each with ample time to spend together.

Chopin ends the chapter with four stories, one told by each of her principal characters. Each of the characters has been warmed by wine, made comfortable by each other's company, and each remi- nisces about particularly telling episodes. Mr. Pontellier's story is about himself and is humorous and mischievous; the Colonel's likewise con- cerns himself, although more solemnly; and the doctor's tale concerns an "old, ever new" story about a woman, lured briefly away from her husband, but returning sensibly after a few days. Edna's tale is quite different. She tells about a pair of young lovers who drift away in a canoe into the southern night, "drifting into the unknown," never to be heard of again. She tells it with such purity and passion that everyone present is moved; its aftermath is strangely akin to the way the summer vacationers on Grand Isle felt after old Mademoiselle Reisz played Chopin's powerful piano music.

The leave-taking of Edna's father is not pleasant. He insists that Edna attend her sister's wedding, and she refuses to do so; he threatens that neither of her sisters will probably speak to her, and he is cer- tain that the bride-to-be will not accept "any excuse." It is at this point that Chopin inserts one of her stylistic gems; still speaking about the outrage of Edna's father, Chopin notes that he assumes that Edna has given an excuse as to why she isn't coming back to Kentucky; the old Colonel is "forgetting that Edna had offered none." This has been characteristic of Edna ever since she decided to have no more "Tuesdays at home." She offers no excuses; Edna is straightforward and frank in her reactions. For that reason, she is often terribly disarming, but she refuses to let herself be compromised by coercion or convention.

Edna's husband, in turn, treats the old Colonel with excessive courtesy; he himself will attend the wedding, hoping that his presence, his "money and love will atone" for what he, we assume, considers to be his childish wife's "mood." Edna's father is as direct as his daughter; he advises Léonce to use authority and coercion on Edna. According to him, they're the "only way to manage a wife"—a subject that has long been just beneath the surface of this novel.

Mr. Pontellier's leaving, which we have been alerted to for some time, occurs shortly after Edna's father departs. While she is packing Léonce's clothing, Edna fears briefly that she may be lonely, but she feels a "radiant peace" when she is at last alone in the house. Even the children are gone, we are told; Léonce's mother has taken them, fearful of her daughter-in-law's lack of maternal indulgence and anxious for their young company, anxious to keep alive in them the Creole ways and temperament.

When Chopin describes Edna's feelings and actions after Léonce leaves, it is as though she were describing the inner thoughts of a person who has just been released from prison. Edna, after "a big, genuine sigh of relief," tours the house, sitting in various chairs and lounges; the house, without Léonce, is like a new acquaintance. She immediately brings in big bouquets of bright flowers and plays with the children's small dog. Edna fills her solitude with the satisfaction she feels within herself. We feel that there is a sense of beginning over, of a new awakening. Edna is enjoying, for the first time, talking with the cook and dining alone, comfortably, in a peignoir. Even the dog seems to be aware of the change within Edna, who is delighted and astonished by her new joy. As the chapter ends, Edna has a long refreshing bath and washes herself clean of old frustrations, of Léonce's interference, and her father's demands. She is "determined to start anew . . . now that her time was completely her own . . . a sense of restfulness invaded her, such as she had not known before."

CHAPTERS 25–32

This section contains many of the novel's most revealing revelations about Edna Pontellier. Following Léonce's departure and her own initial exuberance, Edna becomes restless and moody – filled not with despair, but with boredom, with a sense that "life was passing [her] by." She is a woman who has recently been awakened by romance and love and has declared her independence to paint, but her "art" is not enough to fill her long days; she is aware that she has no real artistic ambitions and that she is not driven by a need for accomplishment.

She fills this void by going again and again to the races; she knows horses and likes the thrill of gambling, the excitement and tenseness of the crowd, and the nostalgic memories of Kentucky horses and paddocks. She is as knowledgeable as most of the men at the track about horses, and she knows it. It is this aura of unusual knowledge and power, in addition to Edna's high-colored handsomeness, that arouses the interest of Alcée Arobin when they attend the races by coincidence together, in the company of one of Edna's friends, a Mrs. Highcamp. Arobin catches "the contagion of excitement," Chopin comments, and is drawn to Edna "like a magnet."

Edna is not unaware of this fact, and she does not flirt with Arobin. On the contrary, it is Arobin, the "young man of fashion" who flirts coquettishly with Edna. Edna's conduct is remarkably cool and contained, even though she feels a fever burning within her. After their first day at the races, and after Arobin has driven her home, she is unusually hungry. She munches on some Gruyere cheese and sips from a bottle of beer, while she pokes "at the wood embers on the hearth"; this is as symbolic to Edna as it is to us. Arobin has stirred the embers of passion within Edna, embers from the summer that were kindled within Edna by Robert Lebrun. There is a restlessness within Edna that wants a release from the bounds of the Pontellier garden and from the four walls of her painting atelier. For this reason, Edna decides to allow herself to go to the races with Arobin alone, to invite him for dinner, and to linger afterward. Yet she cannot allow herself to become merely one more of Arobin's conquests, even though his intimate, confessional tone does tempt her.

When Edna is finally alone, she ponders the possibility of having an affair with Arobin – but on her terms. Chopin is not so blunt as this, but then she could not be in her time. Edna cold-bloodedly considers the consequences of having an affair with this "young man of fashion," and it is significant that it is not herself that she worries about. She doesn't worry about her feelings or even her reputation; it would be easy for her, for "Arobin was absolutely nothing to her." Nor does Edna consider Léonce. It is Robert whom she thinks about; her love for him disturbs her, and an affair with Arobin would seem cheap, a little like adultery. She did not marry Léonce because of love, but she does love Robert, and she cannot reconcile these feelings with the temptation to satisfy her physical craving for a sexual affair with young Arobin. She has sent him away, saying that she no longer likes him, but she is sure that she is as much a narcotic to him as he is to her. Her passion is a need she no longer fears fulfilling, but if she chooses to fill its demands, she must be the one to do the choosing.

Later, after Arobin's polite, elaborate note of apology for acting overly bold so soon after they met, the matter of his kissing her hand seems trivial. Of course, he may see her art studio. Edna is convinced that electric though his charm may be, Arobin is no threat to her. Arobin responds on cue, Chopin tells us "with all his disarming naivete." He is aware that beneath Edna's maturity is raw passion — and he is correct. Chopin tells us that Arobin, despite his rather silly subservience and wide-eyed adoration, pleased the "animalism that stirred impatiently within" Edna.

Feeling a need to talk with someone, it is to old Mademoiselle Reisz that Edna now turns; Edna feels a freedom with her that she can express with few other people. Nothing shocks the old pianist. She is not embarrassed that Edna finds her ailing, her neck wrapped in flannel and that Edna did not ask for an invitation. Nor is Edna embarrassed to drink from the old woman's brandy "as a man would have done." There are no ridiculous, "lady-like" preludes to Edna's reason for coming; she announces immediately that she is moving out of Léonce's house and into a small, four-room house around the corner from Léonce. She wants — and needs — a house of her own. Once uttered aloud, however, the fact of Edna's leaving Léonce's house seems too severe, but old Mademoiselle Reisz will not let Edna make any feeble excuses — such as the Pontelliers' house being too large, the servants too much trouble, etc. She makes Edna state aloud that Léonce's house is not *hers*; it is his. Edna says that she has a little money of her own, the promise of more, and she does want a place of her own in addition to a "feeling of freedom and independence."

That afternoon, over a roaring fire in the old lady's stove, over chocolate, Edna resolves "never again to belong to another than herself." This is one half of this section's climax; the other half concerns another letter that Mademoiselle Reisz has received from Robert Lebrun. Even though the old lady knows that it is painful for Edna to read letters that Robert has written to someone else, she shares them with Edna. She is convinced that Robert is in love with Edna and that he is trying to forget her; that is the reason he left so abruptly for Mexico and why he has not written Edna, something he would have done had he considered Edna merely a casual "friend." Mademoiselle Reisz is sure that Robert saw the social consequences, as well as the futility, of his falling in love with Edna. Thus the old woman gives Edna the letter, one that is unlike any of his other ones. In this letter, Robert writes that he is returning to New Orleans – very soon.

The old woman then forces Edna to admit aloud what she has admitted to no one else: that she is indeed in love with Robert Lebrun and that a woman cannot say *why* she loves whomever it is that she loves. Moreover, she does *not* select the man she falls in love with; love is unreasonable because of its very nature. Edna does not know what she will do when Robert returns. For the present, the mere fact that he is returning is enough. Irrationally, generously, she orders a huge box of bonbons for the children in Iberville. Likewise, her exuberance causes her to write to Léonce; because of Robert's welcome news, Edna is able to break the news of her impending move in a letter to her husband, including her plans for a large "farewell dinner." Edna believes that her letter is charming, and Chopin assures us that it is; it is "brilliant and brimming with cheerfulness."

That night Edna allows herself to be kissed, by firelight, by Arobin; "it was the first kiss of her life to which her nature had really responded." She is as intoxicated as a child before Christmas who cannot wait to open the packages. She allows Arobin's charms to be a surrogate for Robert, for what she imagines will happen when Robert returns. Passion, like an effervescence, builds within Edna. She is choking with the emotions of anticipation, and she allows Arobin to touch her. She follows her instincts instead of thinking about them. But she does not wholly abandon her rationality. When she kisses Arobin, she *decides* to kiss him, "[clasping] his head, [holding] his lips to hers." The promise of Robert's anticipated passion is tumultuous. Edna satisfies her craving, and even Arobin is probably aware that

Edna's thoughts are not about him, for he told her earlier in the evening that he felt as though her thoughts were "wandering, as if they
were not here with me." He was far more accurate than he would
ever have believed, or than his ego would have allowed him to believe.

Inserted into this short scene is an observation made by old
Mademoiselle Reisz; touching Edna's shoulder blades, she explained
to her that she was feeling to see if "the little bird would soar above
the level plain of tradition and prejudice." Such a bird would need
"strong wings," she said, adding that it was a "sad spectacle to see the
weaklings bruised, exhausted, fluttering back to earth." The old
woman senses Edna's strong determination to become something more
than Léonce Pontellier's "property," but the old woman cannot imagine how a married woman and a mother of two young children can
successfully cope — even in New Orleans — merely because she is in
love with a man other than her husband.

Irresponsibility, perhaps, is the first feeling which troubles Edna
after Arobin leaves. She can be sure of Léonce's reproach, were he
to find out about her passionate evening with Arobin; but as we have
seen, Léonce has reproached Edna before. Robert's reproach — that can
be matched and overcome by love and understanding. Significantly,
Edna feels no shame nor remorse for letting Arobin kiss her and for
her taking his head and kissing him deeply. It was an act of passion
that she shared with Arobin, not an act of love — and that makes a
vast difference to Edna. She needed Arobin's passion and regrets that
it could not have been, simultaneously, love, but it was not. It was
only that: passion — no more or no less — and Edna felt better afterward: ". . . as if a mist had been lifted from her eyes, enabling her
to look upon and comprehend the significance of life." Passion is a
part of life, and Edna has satisfied her body's need for passion. Life
is not just love — beautiful, lovely romantic love. Life is a "monster
made up of beauty and brutality" — for women, as well as for men.

Chopin must have enjoyed creating the character of Arobin, the
Casanova. She makes him thoroughly charming, certainly handsome,
kind, well-mannered, but, without caricature, she makes him a man
who is rather shallow, who satisfies himself on the sighs and bodies
of married women until they become uninteresting and a new pros-
pect appears before him. His "conquest" of Edna contains all the little
things that might cause him to believe that Edna is yet another lonely,
idle rich wife who is so captivated by him that she dares convention

to make love with him—for awhile—until he replaces her with another. Edna's unusually lively conversation with him, the fever burning in her cheeks and eyes at the races, her going to the races with him alone, their sitting beside the fire together, her responsiveness to his boyish frankness and boastings, her allowing him to kiss her hand, and then her boldly making love to him—all these things have convinced him that *he* has "stolen her heart" and that when he appears next, he will find her "indulging in sentimental tears."

Arobin could not be more surprised than he is the next day when he finds Edna high atop a ladder, a kerchief knotted around her head, her sleeves rolled to her elbows, looking "splendid and robust," helping a housemaid prepare to take down and pack "everything which she had acquired aside from her husband's bounty." Arobin implores Edna to come down, anxious that she will fall and hurt herself. But Edna refuses. She can barely wait to move to the "pigeon house," as she calls it. There is no recourse for the confused Arobin, since he is a proper gentleman, other than offer to climb up on the ladder himself and unhook the paintings. Edna lets him do this; the offer is convenient. She even makes him don one of her dust caps, which sends the housemaid into "contortions of mirth." The short scene is a brief masterpiece of male-female reversal, filled with the joy of poetic revenge and justice.

Chopin took great care to create interest and suspense about Edna's making one last, grand gesture—a magnificent farewell dinner party. It would be visual, social proof, accompanied by approval and joy, that Edna was "moving out," an artist on her own, maintaining her own lifestyle and her affairs in what she humorously calls the pigeon house. Not surprisingly, however, the party is not the grand affair which Edna fantasized about. We know that Edna has sundered most of her New Orleans social relationships and that she has abandoned her "Tuesdays at home"; logically, New Orleans' social world will not be rocked. The party, as it turns out, is a comfortable group of ten people. Yet Edna has furnished even this small number of people with grandeur and sumptuous magnificance, including a group of hired mandolin players to serenade her guests softly and discretely at a distance from the dining room.

Chopin herself is present, discretely slipping in brief comments about the guests and making us aware that this is a rather odd assemblage of people. For example, we have never heard of the Merrimans until now; we learn that Mr. Merriman is "something of a shallow-pate" and that, because he laughs at other people's witticisms, he is "extremely popular." Arobin is there, of course, over-indulging in flattery for his hostess, and there is also Mrs. Highcamp, a fellow enthusiast of the races. Old Mademoiselle Reisz is wearing fresh violets in her hair, and she is seated, because of her diminutive size, atop a number of plump cushions. Monsieur Ratignolle is alone (his wife fears that she will soon begin labor pains). The aging Miss Mayblunt inspects her food and the other guests through a lorgnette and is said to be intellectual. There is also a "gentleman by the name of Gouvernail . . . of whom nothing special could be said"—in short, a motley lot. Representing the Lebrun family is young and handsome Victor Lebrun, who unexpectedly becomes the center of attention at the party and the reason for the party's coming to a quick conclusion.

Edna, of course, looks magnificent as the hostess in a dazzling gold satin gown, with a fall of flesh-colored lace at the shoulders and a cluster of diamonds atop her forehead. Chopin comments on her regal bearing, her sense of being "alone"; Edna, it seems, stands alone, outside the assemblage of her party and is aware that one person is missing—the person she desires most to be there: Robert. Her love for Robert overpowers her precisely when it should not. The party—if it is to be a true celebration of her independence demands that she retain—despite any mishap—a regal air and command as a hostess, but as it turns out, she cannot bear the sight of the handsome Victor, slightly drunk, garbed and garlanded by Mrs. Highcamp as (in Gouvernail's murmured words) ". . . the image of Desire." She cannot bear the sight of him as the embodiment of pagan desire, and neither can she bear to have him begin to sing the "*si tu savais*" (if you only knew) refrain of the song which Robert once sang to her, the song she sings softly to herself for rhapsodic and romantic comfort.

The party's tableau, with Victor as its focus, is shattered almost in slow motion. The wine has lulled the party into semi-drowsiness and no one is unduly alarmed when Edna cries out for Victor to stop his song, nor when she accidentally shatters her wine glass and its contents across Arobin's legs, nor when she rushes to Victor and places her hand over his mouth. The guests make charming small talk and, like the mandolin players, slowly steal away, and Edna is lost amid a "profound stillness."

The "little bird" that Mademoiselle Reisz spoke of earlier is emotionally – and perhaps physically – exhausted. Her nervous energy caused her to do a good deal of preparation for the party herself. But, for the most part, Edna's exhaustion is due to the coinciding of the monumental decision to move out of her husband's house and the unexpected news that Robert Lebrun is returning to New Orleans. Arobin, of course, thinks that it is his overwhelming charm which is preying upon her sensibilities; her passion is afire for him. Edna lets him think whatever he pleases; she does not concern herself unduly with Arobin. For example, he has filled her pigeon house with large bouquets of fresh flowers and, with old Celestine's help, distributed them everywhere as a surprise for Edna. Edna does not even comment on the flowers. She sits and rests her head on a table and asks Arobin to leave. Instead, he comes to her and smoothes her hair, his hand caressing her bare shoulders, kissing her lightly there, and continuing to caress her until "she had become supple to his gentle, seductive entreaties." Once again, he imagines that it is he and his touch that are causing Edna's anguish. He imagines that he is irresistible and that he can have any woman he chooses. Edna, however, allows him to caress her because she lets herself enjoy what he is a master of.

Emotionally, Edna knows that Arobin is nothing to her. With her head on her arm, her eyes closed, Arobin is simply a stimulus to ease and arouse and please her; her nerves are tense and his touch is tender. Besides, Edna is confident that if Arobin were to become too aggressive, she could tell him to leave and he would do so. She can handle young Arobin – if she chooses to. As noted, she allows him to caress her because her body enjoys – and needs – being touched and soothed. Arobin leaves, feeling triumphant that he has satisfied Edna's passion; little does he fully realize that Edna let herself be aroused by his anonymous, trained touch. With her eyes closed, Edna was scarcely aware of Arobin himself. Her thoughts were with Robert Lebrun.

Léonce Pontellier proves to be far more clever than one might have imagined. When he realizes that his wife seriously means to move out of their house, he invents a ruse of their having their already grand mansion remodeled. The idea is certainly original and certainly ingenious. It is also a surprise when we discover that he does not worry about Edna's moving out causing a personal scandal. On the contrary, Léonce is alarmed about what people might think concerning their "finances." The idea that others might gossip about Edna's moving out being a prelude to Léonce's joining her in the pigeon house almost undoes him. Thus he hires a well-known architect and, within days, the Pontellier house is cluttered with packers, movers, and carpenters – all in an effort to disguise any hint of instability in the Pontellier *fortune*. Léonce's entire concern is with financial scandal; his "unqualified disapproval and remonstrance" are related to the possibility that Edna's latest "whim" might do "incalculable mischief to his business prospects." Chopin's satire on Pontellier's material vanity is superb when she tells us about a brief notice in one of the daily papers (inserted, we can be sure, by Léonce himself) about the possibility that the Pontelliers might spend the summer abroad. Chopin, in her own small way, repays in kind the many years of male laughter over the vanity of women. To be sure, she tips her hand by not suppressing her impulse to include an exclamation point, but who can blame her for summing up Léonce's reaction with ". . . Mr. Pontellier had saved appearances!"

Edna is satisfied with her small house so completely that she soon feels ready to leave it and go see her children, and the week that she spends there is described by Chopin in detail; the paragraphs are full of the "local color" that her critics – prior to the publication of *The Awakening* – were so quick to praise. Edna listens to her little boys' tales of mule riding, fishing, picking pecans, and hauling chips. Even Edna herself enjoys going with them to see the pigs and the cows and also the black servants – laying the cane, thrashing the pecan tree, and catching fish in the back lake. Edna thoroughly enjoys being with the children, answering their questions about the new house – where everyone will sleep and where their favorite toys are. For the entire week, Chopin tells us, Edna gave "all of herself" to her children – unreservedly and happily. And when she has to leave, it is with a sense of regret. All the way home, "their presence lingered with her like the memory of a delicious song." But once Edna returns to New Orleans, her thoughts are not on her children.

This joyous scene of Edna with her children and of her leaving them and returning to New Orleans helps us understand what Edna meant when she told her friend Adèle Ratignolle that she would die for her children, but that she would not give up a life of her own in exchange for a daily devotion to them. Edna loves her children; of that there is no doubt, but she cannot make her family the focus of her life. She admires Adèle's beautiful embodiment of the mother-woman role, but she herself cannot compromise for the stifling demands of the role. Edna does not want a predefined role, and her options seem to be either a mother-woman like Adèle or an eccentric, living only for her art, like old Mademoiselle Reisz. Like her children, Edna's art can richly consume her time, but Edna has no ambition to be a great artist. She doesn't want to be a "dedicated artist," in the same way that she defies being a "dedicated mother" and, especially, a "dedicated wife." The allegiance to the world of "art" is ultimately as unacceptable as the world of "mother, wife, and house-keeper." When Edna decides to move out of the big house into a house of her own, she has no role model to follow. She is aware of the solitude that accompanies her decisions and actions. She has no man to talk with that might offer understanding or direction, nor does she have any other woman – save Adèle and Mademoiselle Reisz – to share her feelings with. Chopin's ending Chapter 32 with the simple sentence "She was again alone" is a clear, direct summing up of Edna's predicament. She is very much alone. Not only now, but ever since her first moments of her awakening, solitude has accompanied her growth. On Grand Isle, she especially felt the embodiment of this solitude in the sea. For that reason, she was supremely happy when she learned to swim in it and no longer had to fear it and have a "hand nearby"; she could freely share in its abundant solitude.

CHAPTERS 33-39

Robert Lebrun's actual return to New Orleans is as surprising to us as it is to Edna. During Edna's dinner party, Victor mentioned nothing about his brother's leaving his job in Mexico; Madame Lebrun has said nothing definite to Edna, nor has Adèle Ratignolle. We know from his letter that Robert plans to return, but we are as shocked as Edna is when she is sitting alone in Mademoiselle Reisz' apartment one evening, waiting for her to come home, and Robert suddenly opens the door.

Coincidentally, one of the reasons that Edna has come to see Mademoiselle Reisz is to talk about Robert. Even though Robert has been gone for almost a year, he has not written to Edna – not even once. As a result, he has become somewhat of a fantasy lover to Edna. She has no certain hope for his returning permanently to New Orleans, so she has filled her stray moments by romantically imagining his returning for a brief visit. Always in her fantasies, Robert has come to her and declared his love for her; or else, in another fantasy, he has accidentally revealed his love for her. Either way, his love for Edna has matched her deep love for him.

Now, however, he is suddenly, physically, before her, and the situation evokes a phrase that Edna used not long ago to describe life; she called it a "monster of beauty and brutality." Reality has come crashing down upon fantasy; the rendezvous she fantasized has occurred and it is the antithesis of how Edna hoped it would be. Robert is as handsome as ever, but he is ill at ease and awkward. When he sits on the piano stool, one of his arms crashes discordantly across the piano keys. The noise is brutal, as is his confession that he has been in New Orleans for two days. Edna's movements in this scene are mechanical, awkward, and unsteady. She has been caught completely off-guard; this is not the way it should have happened. She came to Mademoiselle Reisz' apartment for peace and some solace after a boring, irritating morning, and Robert (her fantasy of peace) has broken her quiet revery.

In the midst of this sudden "brutality" of life, the shattering of all her romantic daydreams, there is also beauty, however, for in spite of Robert's not writing to her, Edna finds in his eyes the tenderness she saw long ago on Grand Isle. Now she finds "added warmth and entreaty," qualities that were not there before. In his eyes, she sees the warmth that kept alive her love for him, the love she sensed was shared between them. Here is the proof—in his eyes.

Yet even this discovery becomes ultimately painful because Robert refuses to acknowledge his feelings for her. Instead, he speaks about settling in with his old firm and ambiguously excuses his not writing by saying that there "have been so many things . . ." Robert has obviously asked a great many questions about Edna. He knows, for example, that the Pontelliers might spend the summer abroad and that Edna has moved into her small house. He seems as shy as Edna is bold. He dares not to do what she has done—that is, face herself and life, with all its "beauty and brutality" and cope with, if not solve, life's problems. Robert has committed himself to the role of becoming a proper New Orleans gentleman and businessman, as Adèle Ratignolle and Mademoiselle Reisz have committed themselves to their prescribed roles. Edna cannot bear the fraudulence she finds in Robert. When he says that his letters would not have been "of any interest" to Edna, the lie is too painful and too insulting. ". . . it isn't the truth," Edna says, and prepares to go. She has waited too long, anticipated too much, fantasized too freely, and now when she is confronted with the man she loves most, she cannot and will not listen to lies or excuses. She has become a fervent disciple of a new integrity, and she will not abide hypocrisy, especially from Robert.

When Robert insists on accompanying her home, she allows him to do so because, after all, Edna is human. She loves him and she has missed him. He begs to stay a bit if Edna will "let" him. The tension between them is broken, and Edna is able to laugh and relax and put her hand on his shoulder and tell him that he is beginning to seem like the old Robert she once knew.

This intimate mood is broken almost immediately, however, when Robert finds a picture of Arobin and is jealous that Edna has it. Edna is neither ashamed nor embarrassed by the picture. Arobin is nothing to her; we know that. Edna tried to make a sketch of Arobin, and he brought the photograph, hoping that it might help her sketching. The photograph is no "lover's gift," no memento. Edna tells Robert no more or no less than the truth: she finds Arobin's head worth drawing, he is a friend of hers, and of late she's come to know him better. Robert calls Edna "cruel" for being so blunt. Edna is not cruel; quite simply, she can play games no longer. Robert grew up playing games; the Creoles all play games. When Edna met Robert, he was playing the role of a knight in search for a fair lady to serve during the summer. In fact, everyone Edna knows plays role games—speaking and acting predictably—and no one questions the role or varies from its prescribed actions. Yet Edna was "awakened," and she questioned her role as wife and mother; afterward, she began to try and fashion a life that would be uniquely hers—something no one she knows has ever done before. Where it will end, she cannot imagine, but she will not compromise—not now, not even with Robert, the man she loves. If Edna is cruel, it is because she has recognized and accepted the fact that life is beautiful and that it is also cruel. If Robert is ever to mature, he too must make his own odyssey, searching for his own truths as thoroughly as Edna has done.

A certain coolness comes between Edna and Robert; Chopin terms it "a certain degree of ceremony." Edna is not able to penetrate Robert's reserve and his reluctance to admit his emotional feelings toward her.

He admits to forgetting "nothing at Grand Isle," but this statement is cautious and non-commital. In contrast, Edna says that being with Robert "never tires" her. He does not comment on this. During the dinner and afterward, Edna is patient with Robert's aloofness until she notices a strikingly embroidered tobacco pouch that Robert lays upon the table. She admires the needlework, and when Robert reveals that the pouch was given to him by a Mexican girl, Edna becomes uncharacteristically jealous. Her questions are uncharacteristically indirect and bitter, and Robert's answers are taunting and ambiguous; behind all of Edna's questions is one single, unasked question: did you love the Mexican girl who gave you the tobacco pouch?

As Robert is pocketing the pouch, Arobin enters. The scene is already bristling with intensity, and Arobin's entrance multiplies that tenseness. When Arobin discovers Robert with Edna, he and Edna perform an impromptu charade of camaraderie, ridiculing Robert's romantic luck with women. Robert's demeanor is seemingly unruffled; he shakes hands with both Edna and Arobin, asks to be remembered to Mr. Pontellier, and leaves. His mentioning Mr. Pontellier is only proper good manners, of course, but it is Robert's subtle way of reminding Edna and Arobin that Edna is a *married* woman.

The next morning's sunlight cheers Edna; after the previous night's confusion and brooding, Edna feels that she was foolish to have been so introspective and jealous. Robert loves her; she was certain of that yesterday and she is just as certain of that today. It is only a matter of time before Robert's reserve is broken—for two reasons: first, because he does love her; and second, because of her passion for him. Edna is convinced that Robert knows that she loves him; soon, he will also realize that she desires him, that he has awakened sexual passion within her. She confronts the possibility of his remaining cool and distant for awhile, but she can live with that possibility. The important thing now is that he *has* returned, that he lives in New Orleans, and is not almost a continent away. Time will awaken Robert; Edna can wait.

Because of her decision to allow Robert his freedom to adjust once again to the business of living in New Orleans and to adjust to the new circumstances of her freedom, Edna is able to deal decisively with the morning's mail. To her son who asks for bonbons, she promises treats; to Léonce, Edna is diplomatic and friendly, though evasive;

she has made no plans to go abroad. In fact, she has made no plans whatsoever. She is absolutely open to whatever Fate offers.

Edna burns Arobin's love note; his professed concern for her is of no consequence. She does allow him, however, to fill her empty hours when days go by and Robert does not call or even send a note. Arobin is allowed to be a surrogate. He possesses a sense of danger and romance and fulfills her need for male companionship. Arobin, meanwhile, preys on Edna's "latent sensuality." And whereas earlier, she often went to bed despondent because Robert had not called, at least now, when Arobin fills her evenings, there is no despondency when she falls alseep, but neither is there a freshness and joy when she awakens in the morning.

Thus Edna lives on the periphery of hope, longing to see Robert and compromising for Arobin's ready, romantic companionship. For that reason, she often goes alone to a small enclosed garden cafe, where she can be alone, can read quietly, and dream idly of Robert. Yet, quite by accident, Robert walks into the garden one day and interrupts her reverie. They are awkward, apologetic, and then distant. Edna attempts to explain why all of her questions to him must seem "unwomanly": she has changed. She says what she thinks now, and she asks questions, and she is prepared to face the consequences. Robert is obviously attracted to her, but he is cautious before this new woman he has discovered. He follows her home, although she does not ask him to do so, and he stays, sitting in the shadows while she goes to bathe her face. When she returns, she leans down and kisses him.

Edna continues to satisfy her passion, putting her hand to his face and pressing her cheek against his. They kiss and he confesses to having wanted to kiss her many times. It was his love for her that drove him away from Grand Isle. He had no other choice.

Edna tries to explain that it makes no difference to her if she is married to Léonce Pontellier. She jokes that Léonce is generous; perhaps he might "give" her to Robert, an offer she finds absurd. No one can "give her away." Edna already *is* free. She belongs to no one except herself. When Robert mentions wanting her to be his wife, she is affronted; she scoffs at "religion, loyalty, everything . . ." Kissing Robert on the eyes, the cheeks, and the lips, she chides him for imagining that someone must "set her free" in order for them to be able to make love.

At that moment a message is delivered, and fate interrupts their passionate avowals. Long ago, Edna promised Adèle to help her when her labor pains began; now Edna must go to her friend. The two lovers kiss goodbye, and Edna feels that Robert's passion matches her own. She promises him that *nothing* is of consequence now – except their love for each other. She leaves him precisely when he needs her most. Robert is weak; he needs Edna's strength. He fully realizes how thoroughly he loves this married woman who promises herself, who promises to defy all convention for him.

Witnessing Adèle in the throes of childbirth is painful for Edna. The physical pain she sees is symbolic of the psychological pain she feels is inherent in motherhood. This scene of birth is ugly and bloody and preludes, for Edna, Adèle's never-ending bondage to a child who will overpower her will and identity. And Adèle will allow it to happen. Edna cannot. The scene causes Edna to remember her own painful scenes of childbirth and her "awakening to find a little new life she had been given." But Edna has awakened now as an adult and found a new little life that she herself created – and this new life is liberating. It does not limit; being a mother limits one, and the pain Edna sees before her is not as painful as the fact that once one has decided to become a mother-woman, one gives up everything for the children. Despite the torture that Edna sees Adèle enduring, torture and pain which Edna finds repulsive, Edna stays – in revolt and as a witness against nature for its cruel demands. She stays so long, in fact, that Adèle is able to whisper, exhaustedly, that Edna should "think of the children . . . think of the children! Remember them!" Adèle, even in her great pain, is thinking of Edna, afraid that Edna is about to abandon her husband and children in exchange for a romantic whim. She appeals to what she, as a mother, holds most sacred: the children, even as she suffers the pains of birth.

For Adèle, this new baby is new evidence of her worth as a mother-woman; for Edna, it is yet another burden; it is a reminder of a woman's powerlessness, of how her liberty is checked by men, family, and society.

When Edna is free at last of the confines of the Ratignolle's apartment, she feels dazed; the trauma of seeing her friend give birth has unnerved her. Even Doctor Mandelet thinks it was cruel for Adèle to insist that Edna witness the childbirth scene in order that she might recall that she too had once given birth, that she too had brought forth children from her body, and that they were, by definition, physical extensions of herself. They grew within her body and despite their being severed, they are still part of her flesh and blood.

The object lesson was not wholly lost on Edna. Before she left for Adèle's house, she was convinced that no one would, or could, or should, demand that she do anything she did not wish to do. Now she is not sure. She *is* sure that Léonce cannot force her to go abroad, but she is unable to say, unreservedly, that no one has the right to force her to do anything that she does not wish to do "except children, perhaps . . ." Her thoughts are incoherent.

Yet of one thing she is sure; she has awakened to new visions and new perspectives and new possibilities, and she can never return to a life of dreaming and illusions or of being Mrs. Léonce Pontellier. Motherhood, in contrast, has become nebulous; *her* life should come first; she should be able to live her life her way – regardless of whom she must "trample upon," and yet, ultimately, she realizes that she cannot "trample upon the little lives."

We have never seen Edna, for any length of time, exhibit maternal feelings. Her children and her love for them have been vague and on the periphery of this novel, except for the week spent at their grandmother's home. Yet witnessing Adèle give birth has made Edna realize anew that her children were created within her own body and that a mother must, ultimately, be responsible for them.

At the same time, she can envision no greater bliss than that which she shared with Robert – their embracing, their kissing and expressing their love for one another. He almost gave himself to her. She resolves to think of the children tomorrow. She will awaken Robert's passion again tonight with her kisses and arouse him with her caresses. There will be time to think of the children tomorrow. Tonight she will awaken Robert and claim him.

But Robert is not waiting for her. He has left a note saying goodbye. He leaves her because he loves her. She has been willing to sacrifice everything – even the little ones – for him, but he is afraid to risk anything.

The final chapter of the novel is set once again on Grand Isle. Robert's brother, Victor, is patching up one of the cottages and the feisty, flirtatious Mariequita is sitting in the sun watching him, handing him nails and dangling her legs. Victor has talked for an hour of nothing but the fabulous party at Edna's; he has described in exaggerated detail the party, embroidering his memories with romantic fancy, especially his memory of Edna, resplendent in sparkling diamonds. Both young people are struck dumb with amazement when Edna suddenly appears and begins to chatter about hearing the hammering and being glad to know that the loose planking is being mended, complaining how dreary and deserted everything looks. She has come to rest, she says; any little corner will do. She is alone and simply needs to get away and rest.

The young people continue to chat and argue, while Edna walks toward the beach; she does not hear them. The sun is hot and she lets its heat penetrate her. Edna has reached a crisis, one which she must solve alone. She has no man she can relate to; Robert is gone. Léonce does not matter. She has no woman she can relate to: Adèle's role of mother-woman is as oppressive and limited as old Mademoiselle Reisz's role as an artist. Edna's priorities demand that she cannot compromise her newly awakened life for anyone. All of her friends have safe, well-defined niches, but those niches have walls; the old-fashioned, rosy ideals of marriage and motherhood are rank to Edna. The absurdity of condemning herself to such tyranny is too much to ask.

As she enters the sea, she cuts cleanly through the waves and begins to swim out farther than any woman has ever gone before. Here, there are no goals, no roles, no boundaries; there is only the solitude that whispered to her long ago. There is a freshness in the sea that is denied her in the Pontellier house; as a wife and mother, she would stagnate, losing all self-confidence and direction; thus she chooses to swim out to her death. Already, of course, metaphorically she has swum out further than any woman has done when she risked enticing Robert to a romance that would preclude her roles of wife and mother. Edna knows what she is rejecting. Never again will she be bound into a role that she does not choose for herself.

She hears the sea and its murmurs; they seem to be "inviting the soul to wander in abysses of solitude." Edna's solitude is her own companion. Robert, especially, has abandoned her. Above, a bird with a broken wing, beats the air, fluttering, circling, until it reels down the water." Mademoiselle Reisz warned Edna once, using the symbol of a little bird, about having the strength and courage to be able to fly if one were to "soar above the level plain and prejudice . . ." At that time, the old woman felt Edna's shoulder blades to see if Edna's "wings were strong." It was a sad spectacle, she said, to see the weaklings "bruised, exhausted, fluttering back to earth."

Yet the bird Edna watches does not fall to the earth; it falls into the sea. And Edna does not die "bruised" and "fluttering." She enters the water naked, swimming where "the waves . . . invited her." There is no sense of melodrama and hysteria here. Edna lets the sea "caress her, enfold her" in its "soft, close embrace." These are words of love and passion. Edna listens to its voice, and she understands its depths of solitude. She knows that this is no shallow haven of simple calm. This is a deep, restless sea of change and currents. She is not afraid, even though her arms and legs are tiring. No one can claim her now; she can give herself to the sea. And she does, freely joining her solitude with its own solitude. She had to choose and decide whether or not life was worth being lived on terms other than her own, and she decided that it was not. She confronted life's most fundamental philosophical question. That act was an "awakening" in itself. She acts in revolt against the tyranny she finds in social myths that would limit her growth as a free woman. She cannot find meanings in the family unit as it exists and to accept the sacred connotations that generations have given to it would be living fraudulently. The quality of short experience that Edna finds swimming out to her death is measureless, compared to the endless years of robot-like role playing which she would be condemned to were she to return to Léonce Pontellier and her family. Edna's awakening on Grand Isle gives her no alternative. Swimming out to her death gives Edna a sense of dignity because the choice is hers. She has grasped the full reality of the hollow life that would be hers if she condemned herself to living "for the little ones." By choosing death, she frees herself from continuing an existence that would be miserably mechanical. She cuts off all hope for herself by choosing death, but she can conceive of no real hope otherwise. Freedom is more important, even in these few short minutes that she swims out. It is a strange, new clarity that Edna possesses. Her last thoughts are of her youth, the time prior to her awakening. She returns to this state of purity, free of a world that would encase her and consume her. Edna's strokes in the sea are "long, sweeping"; they are not "frantic beatings." We must, of necessity, imagine her as happy and free at last.

QUESTIONS FOR REVIEW

1. What is Grand Isle? Where is it, geographically, in relation to New Orleans?

2. How much older is Mr. Pontellier than Edna? How long have they been married, and what is the significance of their age difference?

3. Describe Edna's physical appearance and her character at the beginning of the novel.

4. What are the circumstances of Edna's first "awakening"? Would you describe Edna's "awakening" as happy or unhappy? Explain.

5. Describe Robert Lebrun's charm early in the novel. Why does he finally decide to leave Edna?

6. Characterize the Creole women, in contrast to Edna.

7. Why does Robert decide to go to Mexico?

8. Mademoiselle Reisz' lifestyle is one of the choices Edna considers after her "awakening." Describe this particular lifestyle.

9. What kind of a mother is Edna? What kind of a hostess is she for her husband?

10. Is Chopin sympathetic to Alcée Arobin? Why or why not?

11. What is Mr. Pontellier's reaction to Edna's announcement that she is moving into the pigeon house?

12. Describe Edna's relationship with Arobin.

13. Briefly comment on the conclusion and the consequences of Edna's grand party.

14. How does Edna finally come to view life? How is this viewpoint different from her viewpoint at the beginning of the novel? Explain the term "life's delirium."

15. How does Adèle's childbirth scene affect Edna?

16. What importance does Chopin assign to the sea in this novel?

17. In your own words, paraphrase Edna's reasons for committing suicide. Do you agree or disagree with her? Explain.

SELECTED BIBLIOGRAPHY

BERTHOFF, WARNER. *The Ferment of Realism: American Literature 1884-1919.* New York: Free Press, 1965.

BUTCHER, PHILIP. "Two Early Southern Realists in Revival," *College Language Association Journal,* 14 (1970), 91-95.

EATON, CLEMENT. "Breaking a Path for the Liberation of Women in the South," *Georgia Review,* 28 (Summer, 1974), 187-99.

EBLE, KENNETH. "A Forgotten Novel: Kate Chopin's *The Awakening,*" *Western Humanities Review,* X (Summer 1956), 261-69.

FLETCHER, MARIE. "Kate Chopin's Other Novel," *Southern Literary Journal,* 1 (August 1966), 60-74.

_____. "The Southern Women in the Fiction of Kate Chopin," Louisiana Historical Quarterly, 7 (Spring, 1966), 117-32.

MAY, JOHN R. "Local Color in *The Awakening,*" *Southern Review,* 6 (1970) 1031-40.

LEARY, LEWIS. "Introduction," *The Awakening and Other Stories.* New York: Holt, Rinehart and Winston, Inc., 1970.

_____. "Kate Chopin and Walt Whitman," *Walt Whitman Review,* XVI (December 1970), 120-21.

_____. "Kate Chopin, Liberationist?" *Southern Literary Journal*, III (Fall 1970), 138-44.

MILLINER, GLADYS W. "The Tragic Imperative: *The Awakening* and *The Bell Jar*," *Mary Wollstonecraft Newsletter*, II (December 1973), 21-26.

OBERBECK, S.K. "St. Louis Woman," *Newsweek*, LXXV (February 23, 1970), 103-04.

POTTER, RICHARD H. "Kate Chopin and Her Critics: An Annotated Checklist," *Missouri Historical Society Bulletin*, XXVI (July 1970), 306-17.

RINGO, DONALD A. "Romantic Imagery in Kate Chopin's *The Awakening*," *American Literature*, 43 (January 1972), 580-88.

ROCKS, JAMES E. "Kate Chopin's Ironic Vision," *Louisiana Review*, I (Winter 1972), 110-20.

ROSEN, KENNETH M. "Kate Chopin's *The Awakening*: Ambiguity as Art," *Journal of American Studies*, 5 (August 1971), 197-200.

SCHUYLER, WILLIAM. "Kate Chopin," *The Writer*, VIII (August 1894), 115-17.

SEYERSTED, PER. *Kate Chopin: A Critical Biography*. Baton Rouge: Louisiana State University Press, 1969.

SKAGGS, MERRILL M. *The Folk of Southern Fiction*. Athens: University of Georgia Press, 1972.

SPANGLER, GEORGE. "Kate Chopin's *The Awakening*: A Partial Dissent." *Novel*, 3 (1970), 249-55.

SULLIVAN, RUTH AND STEWART SMITH. "Narrative Stance in Kate Chopin's *The Awakening*," *Studies in American Fiction*, I (1973), 62-75.

WILSON, EDMUND. *Patriotic Gore: Studies in the Literature of the American Civil War*. New York: Oxford University Press, 1962.

WOLFF, CYNTHIA. "Thanatos and Eros: Kate Chopin's *The Awakening*," *American Quarterly*, XXV (October 1973), 449-71.

ZIFF, LARZER. *The American 1890s: Life and Times of a Lost Generation*. New York: The Viking Press, 1966.

ZLOTNICK, JOAN. "A Woman's Will: Kate Chopin on Selfhood, Wifehood, and Motherhood," *Markham Review*, III (October 1968), 1-5.

Think Quick

Now there are more Cliffs Quick Review® titles, providing help with more introductory level courses. Use Quick Reviews to increase your understanding of fundamental principles in a given subject, as well as to prepare for quizzes, midterms and finals.

Do better in the classroom, and on papers and tests with Cliffs Quick Reviews.

Your Guides to Successful Test Preparation.

Cliffs Test Preparation Guides
• Complete • Concise • Functional • In-depth

Efficient preparation means better test scores. Go with the experts and use *Cliffs Test Preparation Guides*. They focus on helping you know what to expect from each test, and their test-taking techniques have been proven in classroom programs nationwide. Recommended for individual use or as a part of a formal test preparation program.

Publisher's ISBN Prefix 0-8220

Qty.	ISBN	Title	Price	Qty.	ISBN	Title	Price
	2078-5	ACT	8.95		2044-0	Police Sergeant Exam	9.95
	2069-6	CBEST	8.95		2047-5	Police Officer Exam	14.95
	2056-4	CLAST	9.95		2049-1	Police Management Exam	17.95
	2071-8	ELM Review	8.95		2076-9	Praxis I: PPST	9.95
	2077-7	GED	11.95		2017-3	Praxis II: NTE Core Battery	14.95
	2061-0	GMAT	9.95		2074-2	SAT*	9.95
	2073-4	GRE	9.95		2325-3	SAT II*	14.95
	2066-1	LSAT	9.95		2072-6	TASP	8.95
	2046-7	MAT	12.95		2079-3	TOEFL w/cassettes	29.95
	2033-5	Math Review	8.95		2080-7	TOEFL Adv. Prac. (w/cass.)	24.95
	2048-3	MSAT	24.95		2034-3	Verbal Review	7.95
	2020-3	Memory Power for Exams	5.95		2043-2	Writing Proficiency Exam	8.95

Prices subject to change without notice.

Available at your booksellers, or send this form with your check or money order to **Cliffs Notes, Inc.,** P.O. Box 80728, Lincoln, NE 68501 http://www.cliffs.com

☐ Money order ☐ Check payable to Cliffs Notes, Inc.

☐ Visa ☐ Mastercard   Signature_____

Card no. _____ Exp. date _____

Signature _____

Name _____

Address _____

City _____ State_____ Zip_____

*GRE, MSAT, Praxis PPST, NTE, TOEFL and Adv. Practice are registered trademarks of ETS. SAT is a registered trademark of CEEB.

Get the Cliffs Edge

Make the most efficient use of your study time. All it takes is an edge--an edge like study guides from Cliffs. Test Preparation Guides and Cliffs Notes are just two of the publications that can help you excel scholastically.

TEST PREPARATION GUIDES

- Enhanced ACT
- AP Biology
- AP Chemistry
- AP English Language and Composition
- AP English Literature and Composition
- AP U.S. History
- CBEST
- CLAST
- ELM Review
- GMAT
- GRE
- LSAT
- MAT
- Math Review for Standardized Tests

- Memory Power
- NTE Core Battery
- Police Officer Examination
- Police Sergeant Examination
- Postal Examinations
- PPST
- SAT I
- TASP™
- TOEFL
- Advanced Practice for the TOEFL
- Verbal Review for Standardized Tests
- WPE
- You Can Pass the GED

CLIFFS NOTES

More than 200 titles are available. Each provides expert analysis and background of plot, characters and author to make it easier to understand literary masterpieces.

Get the Cliffs Edge!

Cliffs offers a full line of study guides to give you an edge on tests, papers and in classroom discussion. Available wherever books or software are sold or contact: CLIFFS, P.O. Box 80728, Lincoln, NE 68501. Phone: (402) 423-5050.